MACMILLAN SOCIAL STUDIES

My World
Myself and others in my world

Families and Friends
Family and school life

People and Neighborhoods
The neighborhood and local community

Communities Today and Yesterday
Comparison of communities within the United States

The Earth and Its People
Communities in grassland, mountain, desert, polar, tropical, and island regions

The United States and the Other Americas
History and geography of the United States, and of Canada and Latin America

Nations of the World
History and geography of Europe, Asia, Africa, and Australia

World Neighbors
History and geography of countries throughout the world

Macmillan Social Studies

Communities Today and Yesterday

SENIOR AUTHOR
John Jarolimek

Mae Knight Clark

ADAPTED BY
Peg Paul
Sara Rau
Ene Mai Kvell
Rosalie Fleisher
Peggy Teeters

GEOGRAPHY CONSULTANT
Loyal Durand, Jr.

Macmillan Publishing Co., Inc.
New York

Collier Macmillan Publishers
London

Macmillan Publishing Co., Inc.
866 Third Avenue
New York, NY 10022
Collier Macmillan Canada, Inc.

Printed in the United States of America

ISBN 0-02-147940-2

9 8 7 6 5 4

Contents

1

Moving to a New Community, 8

2

Cities as Communities, 76

3

Communities at Work, 142

4

New and Old Communities, 218

Learning About Maps and Globes, 289

Word List, 306

Maps, Charts, and Diagrams

UNIT 1

Moving to a New Community

This book will show you how different people live in our country today. It will also show you how some people lived here long ago. You will learn how people can move to a place where no one lives. You will learn how they make that place into a good place to live.

Looking at the Pictures

The pictures on these pages show places where people live. Look at them carefully.

Which one is most like the place where you live? In what ways is it different?

What places do the other two pictures show?

Which picture shows something from the past? What might you see today in its place?

Looking Ahead

As you read, try to answer these questions:

How, and why, do people live together?
What do people need to live?
How do some people get what they need to live?
How did some people long ago meet their needs?

Words to Watch For

Look at the words below. As you read, you will find out what they mean. You will find out how to say them. Look in the Word List, too.

basic needs	desert	Pilgrims	shelter
community	history	pioneer	

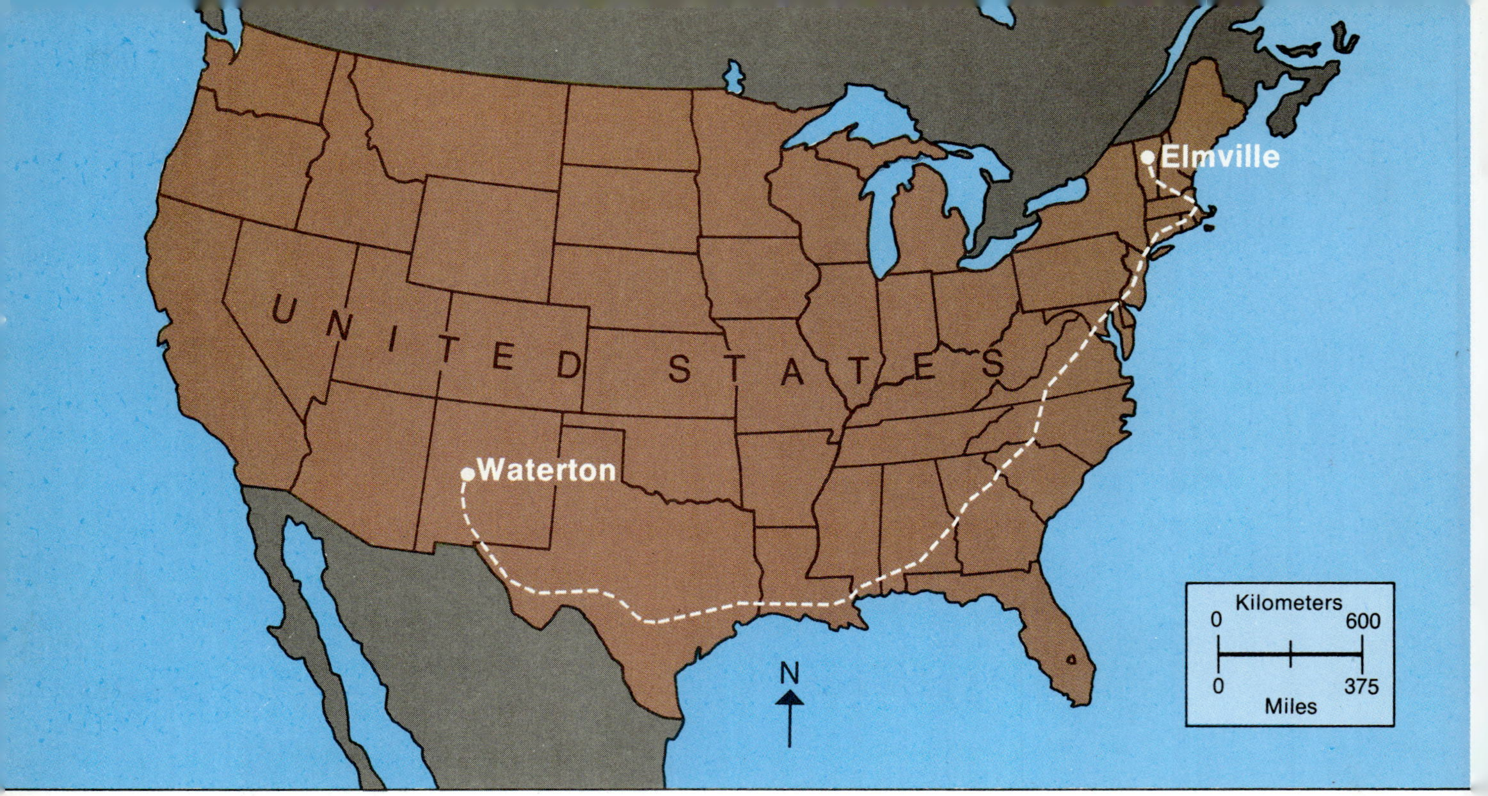

1

What Is a Community?

Lisa and Matt were in the kitchen when their father came home. Lisa was slicing tomatoes for a salad. Her younger brother was putting forks and spoons on the dinner table.

"Where's Mother?" Mr. Roberts asked.

"Outside," Lisa answered. "She's putting photos in the mail."

Mrs. Roberts was a photographer (fə **täg** rə fər). A photographer takes pictures like those in this book.

You will see them as you read along in this book. People who write newspapers and magazines often bought Mrs. Roberts's pictures.

"Matt," Mr. Roberts said, "go ask Mother to come as soon as she can. I have some important news."

Mrs. Roberts came in a few minutes. Her eyes were shining.

"Has it happened at last, Ted?" she asked her husband.

"Yes, Lee. It's time to tell the children."

"What? Tell us what?"

Matt and Lisa crowded around their father, doing a little dance.

"Sit down, and I'll explain," Mr. Roberts said with a laugh.

Vermont has many maple trees.
Farmers get sap from them.

Mr. Roberts took a map from his pocket. He put it on the table and grinned.

Then he said, "We're going to move."

"Where?" asked Matt.

"Why?" asked Lisa.

"When?" asked Mrs. Roberts.

"One at a time!" said Mr. Roberts. "I'll answer all those questions."

A Different Part of the Country

Mr. Roberts told the family that they would soon leave Elmville. In a few weeks they would move to New Mexico. He pointed to Elmville on the map. It was in the state of Vermont. Then he pointed to New Mexico.

This family is camping in New Mexico. How is it unlike Vermont?

Beavers use trees to make *dams.*
Have you ever seen a beaver *dam*?

"It looks like a long way," Lisa said.

"It is a long way," said Mrs. Roberts.

Mr. Roberts also explained why they were going. He worked as an *engineer* (en jə **nēr**) for a large company. Many engineers know how to build *dams.* They make plans for builders to help them build strong dams. Mr. Roberts's company was going to build a dam in New Mexico. Mr. Roberts would help plan the dam.

"What's a dam?" asked Matt.

"Oh, you know," said Lisa. "Remember the beaver dam at Grandpa's farm?"

"Yes," said Matt. "The beaver put logs, sticks, stones, and mud in the stream. Then the water couldn't get by."

The high concrete wall of this *dam* holds back the river's water.

"The water backed up behind the dam," Lisa said. "It made a little lake. A lake is water with land all around it."

"That was fun," said Matt. "But why are you building a dam, Dad?"

"That's a big question," said Mr. Roberts. "Let's have dinner first. After dinner we'll talk some more."

To Be a Pioneer

After dinner, Lisa sat alone on the porch. A breeze cooled the July night. She thought about the move. She thought about leaving Elmville and school. In a few months she would start third grade. Suddenly, she felt Mother's hands on her shoulders.

"A penny for your thoughts," Mrs. Roberts said.

"Oh, Mom," she said, "do we have to go?"

"Yes, dear," her mother said, "we have to go. But we will be coming back when the dam is built. That may take three years or more. In the meantime, we all need to be together."

"I know that," said Lisa, "It's just that I'll have to say goodbye to my friends. And I wanted to be in Ms. Costa's class this year. Last year she gave a party. Her party was for all of us who would be in third grade this year.

"She said we would learn more about Indians and *pioneers* (pī ə **nirz**)."

"What's a pioneer?" asked Matt. He had just run onto the porch.

These *pioneers* crossed our country before automobiles were invented.

"Oh, Matt," said Lisa. "Pioneers lived in America long ago. They lived here when there were a lot of trees and no cities. They left home and came to new lands. They led the way for others to follow."

"Oh, I know," said Matt, "I've seen pioneers on TV. They built log cabins. They traveled in wagons pulled by horses."

"Well," said Mrs. Roberts, "pioneers do lead the way for others. But pioneers didn't live just a long time ago. There are pioneers today, too. And they don't live only in log cabins. After all, we're going to be pioneers in New Mexico."

"Pioneers?" said Lisa. Her eyes opened wider.

"Will there be Indians?" asked Matt.

"Yes," said Mrs. Roberts. "There will be Indians. In fact, you may have school friends who are Indians."

"Will we live in a log cabin?" asked Lisa.

"No," said her mother, "we will live in a mobile home at first. A mobile home is a house on wheels. It will be very comfortable, but we will be pioneers just the same. We will be pioneers of today."

Do You Know?

1. Where does the Roberts family live now?
2. Where will the Roberts family move to?
3. Why is the Roberts family moving?
4. What is a pioneer?

People need water and food to live.
What foods do you see here?

Meeting Basic Needs

Mrs. Roberts explained what it would be like to be a pioneer today. No matter where people are, Mrs. Roberts said, they need certain things to live. They have *basic needs* (**bā** sik **nēdz**). Basic needs are things people must have in order to live.

—People need *shelter* (**shel** tər). Sometimes shelter is called housing.

—People need clothes.

—People need water.

—People need food.

Food, warm clothing, and shelter are needs of winter campers.

Of course, other things are important in life, too. People want to be comfortable. They want to feel safe. They want to have friends and a family. They want to learn about the world. They want to enjoy themselves. But people can live without these things. Basic needs are things people cannot do without.

"Are my toys basic needs?" asked Matt. He thought of one toy he took to school every day.

"No," said his mother. "Toys are fun to play with. But if you didn't have them, you would go right on living."

A *desert* is often an empty place. It is too dry for most living things.

Meeting basic needs was a problem for earlier pioneers. They had to build shelter, find water, hunt for food. They had no cars and no highways. They had no supermarkets and no trailers. Today, we have these things. But meeting basic needs can still be hard.

"The biggest problem in New Mexico," said Mrs. Roberts, "will be getting water."

"Why will water be a problem?" asked Lisa.

"Because we are going to live in a *desert* (**dez** ərt)," said Mrs. Roberts.

What Is a Desert?

Mr. Roberts came out to the porch. Together, the family talked about the desert.

A desert is very dry. Some deserts can be very hot during the day. But, at night, the temperature drops sharply. Night in the desert can be very cool. A desert is covered with rocks, sand, or dry soil. Few trees or plants grow on the desert.

"Why are there so few plants?" asked Lisa.

"Because there isn't enough water," said her mother. "Plants as well as people have basic needs. All living things need water to live and grow."

"Desert soil, or earth, however, is rich," Mr. Roberts added. "With enough water, the desert can be used to grow things. Then it can meet some of our food needs."

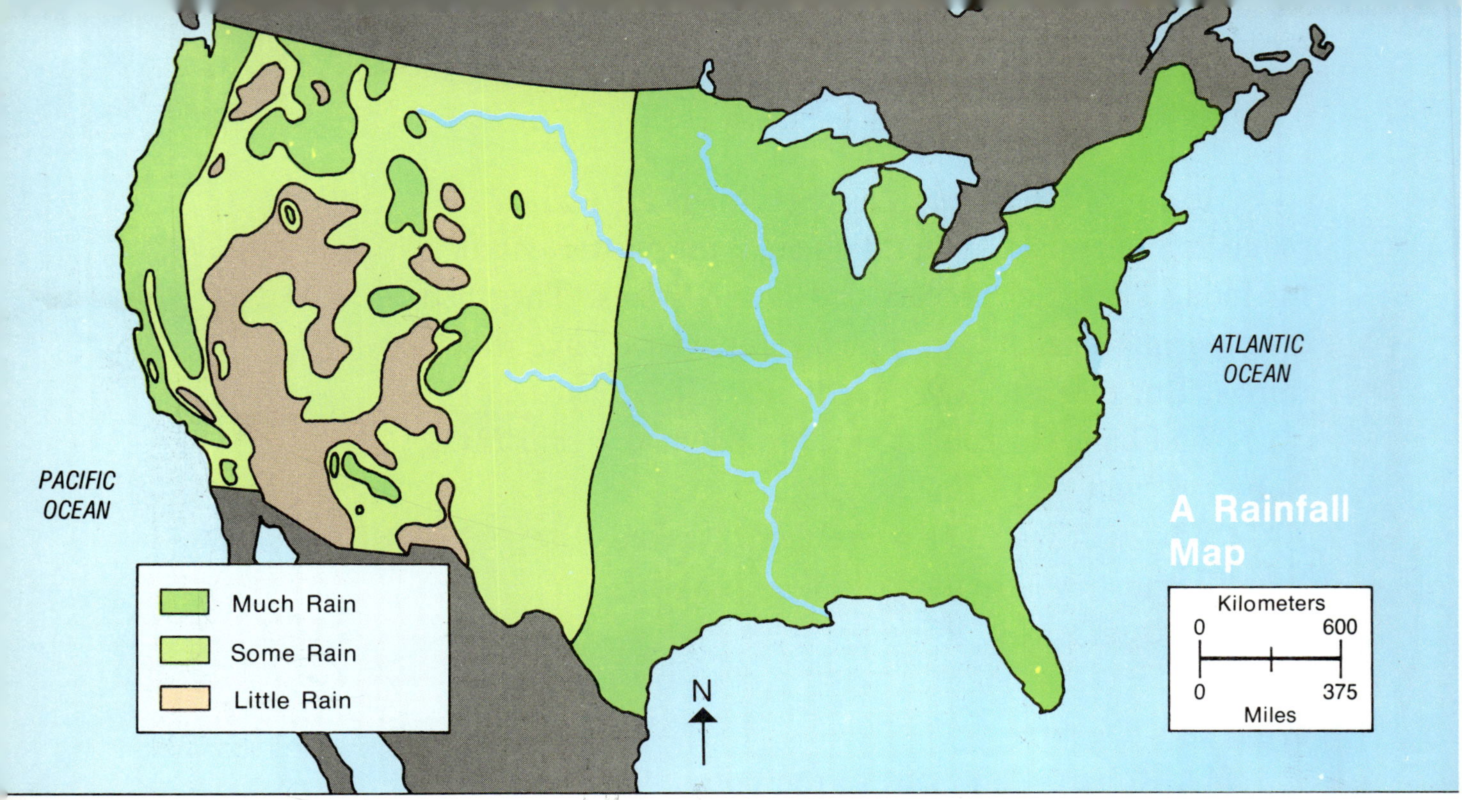

How can water come to a desert? Certainly it does *not* come from rainfall. Look at the rainfall map. You can see that parts of our country get very little rain. Other parts get a lot of rain. In the eastern part of our country, where Elmville is, there is a lot of rain. Trees and plants grow quickly. But, in most of New Mexico, there is very little rain.

Rivers, however, run through the desert in New Mexico. A river carries water from the mountains (**moun** tənz). Near the river, people are able to grow crops. But, in the spring, the river becomes a problem. At that time, snow on top of the mountains melts. This snow becomes water. The water runs down the

A *flood* has come into this farmer's barn. He is saving the cattle feed.

mountains and into the river. Water in the river rises higher and higher. Sometimes there is a *flood* (**flud**).

A flood happens when water flows over the banks, or sides, of a river. The water covers fields and kills crops. Sometimes it makes the earth salty. It may be many years before crops can grow again. Sometimes floods cover houses. Floods even wash houses away.

"Isn't it strange," said Mrs. Roberts, "for most of the year the land is too dry. Then, in the spring, the river brings floods. Both too much water and too little water are bad for crops."

"What can the people do?" asked Lisa.

"They can build a dam," said Mrs. Roberts.

What Dams Do

Mrs. Roberts was right. Dams can help people solve the problem of too much or too little water.

Workers build dams across rivers. Water is held behind the dam. The water becomes a lake. When snow melts, the lake fills with water. When summer comes, the water is let out of the dam slowly. Just enough water comes onto the land each day. In that way, crops get enough water all the time. Getting water to crops this way is called *irrigation* (ir ə **gā** shən). Most crops that are raised in deserts get their water through irrigation.

"Now you know why I'm going to help build a dam," said Mr. Roberts.

"Yes," said Matt. "You're going to stop the floods."

"And," said Lisa, "your dam will bring water to the crops."

"What about the plants and animals?" asked Mrs. Roberts. "I've read that dams can sometimes harm them."

"That's true," said Mr. Roberts. "Dams sometimes harm living things. Today, dams are planned. People study the place where the dam will be built. If they see any danger to plants or animals, they report it. The facts are looked at. Then it is decided whether or not to build the dam."

Water can be brought to *crops* through pipes or ditches.

Do You Know?

1. Why is a desert dry?
2. How can a dam help make crops grow?
3. Why do people study the places where dams are to be built?

Things To Do

1. Read a story about pioneer life. Tell it to the class.
2. Make a list of your "basic needs." What other things do you want?

Travel Plans

In the last two weeks of July, the Roberts family planned its trip. Mr. Roberts took out his map. The family decided which places they would visit. They would drive their car to New Mexico. It would be a vacation as well as a family move. They would take a whole month to see a lot of our country on the way.

My Trip List

DAY WE ARRIVE	DAY WE LEAVE	PLACES WE WILL VISIT
August 1	August 3	Plymouth, Massachusetts
August 3	August 8	New York City
August 8	August 13	Washington, D.C.
August 13	August 15	Smoky Mountains
August 15	August 18	Atlanta, Georgia
August 18	August 25	New Orleans, Louisiana
August 25	August 28	Austin, Texas
August 29	September 1	El Paso, Texas
September 1		Trailer camp, New Mexico

Mrs. Roberts helped Lisa make a trip list. They wrote down all the places they would visit. They wrote down when they would arrive and when they would leave. Look at the trip list on page 26. When did the Robertses plan to leave Elmville? When did they plan to get to New Mexico?

Mrs. Roberts was very excited about making this trip.

"Our trip makes me think about my old job," she said. "Before you children were born I worked for a newspaper. I traveled to many parts of our country to take pictures. I even went to Canada."

"Oh, let's pretend to be reporters," Lisa said. She knew that reporters often go to many different places. They talk to many people. Then they write about those places and people.

"I can't write yet," said Matt sadly.

Mrs. Roberts gave him a hug. "You can certainly ask a lot of questions, though. And all reporters must ask questions. Maybe you can pretend to be a TV reporter."

What a Community Is

One evening, Lisa's father said to her, "What does Elmville mean to you?"

"My teacher last year called Elmville a *community* (kə **mū** nə tē)," she said.

"What's a community?" asked Matt.

Each *community* is a special place.
It can be big, small, old, or new.

"A community," Lisa said, "is a place where people live close together. It is a place that helps people meet their needs."

"Are all communities like Elmville?" Matt asked.

Mr. Roberts explained that there are many kinds of communities. Some may be small towns like Elmville. Others may be large places like New York City or Chicago. Many early pioneers built communities. So did the Indians, the very first people to come to our land. The new mobile home park in New Mexico would be a community, too.

"Elmville will always be my favorite community," said Lisa.

"Why not do something special to help you remember Elmville?" Mrs. Roberts asked. "Make a list of all the ways that Elmville helps people," said her mother. "Be sure to include how it helps us meet our basic needs. Then think how it has other things that we may want as well. After all, you may not need movies and cookies to live. But they help make your life fun. That's what I mean by things we want."

Lisa made her list. At the same time, Mrs. Roberts took pictures of the things on Lisa's list. She made those pictures into a photo story. A photo story is a group of pictures arranged to tell a story. You will see several photo stories in this book.

The list Lisa made is on page 32. Mrs. Roberts's photo story about Elmville is on pages 30 and 31.

A Small Community Meets Its Needs

Look at the pictures to see how the people of Elmville live.

How do they meet their needs?

Describe how they enjoy themselves.

Would people living in a large city do the things you see here in different ways?

A PROCLAMATION

Lisa's List

THE COMMUNITY OF ELMVILLE

1. Elmville has houses for people to live in. There are big houses and small houses. Usually one family lives in each house.
2. Elmville has a shopping center where you can buy food and clothing. It also has a lumber yard.
3. Elmville has good roads and schools.
4. The Elmville newspaper is printed once a week. There is one movie theatre.
5. Elmville has a fire truck. When a fire breaks out, people hurry to the station. Elmville also has a police station. Elmville has two churches.
6. Elmville has doctors, nurses, and a small hospital.
7. Elmville has a town meeting once a year. At that meeting, people talk about town needs. They make laws for the town.

Do You Know?

1. What are communities?
2. How are Elmville and large cities alike?
3. What happens at Elmville's town meetings?
4. What is a photo story?

To Help You Learn

Using New Words

basic needs	engineer	pioneers
community	flood	shelter
dam	irrigation	town meeting
desert		

Do you know the meanings of the words above?

These words are used in the part of the book you have just read. The first time a new word is used in this book, it is explained. The new word is printed in a different, slanted kind of type. This will help you see it.

For example, turn to page 14. Find the word *dams*. Notice that it looks different from the other words. See what its meaning is.

Find in your book all of the words listed above. Read the sentence in which each is first used.

Now, make up your own sentence, using each word in the list.

Talking It Over

1. Will the Roberts family's basic needs change after they leave Elmville? Why? Why not?
2. In what ways are the Robertses going to be pioneers?
3. Why do you think people live in communities?
4. How is the dam going to change the desert?

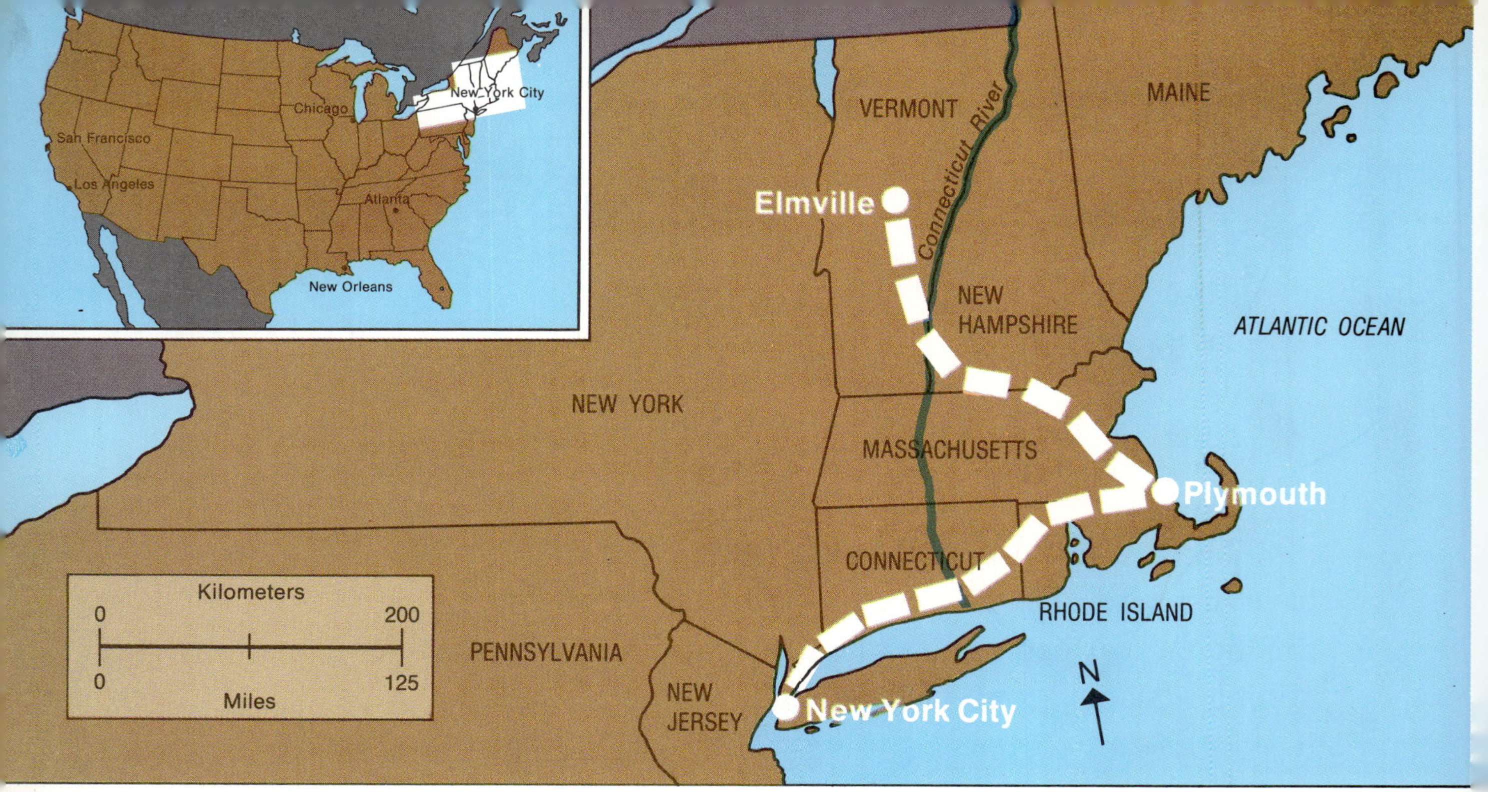

2

Early Communities of the Woodlands

The day for leaving Elmville had finally come. Friends gathered around the station wagon to say goodbye. As the Robertses drove away, they all became quiet. Each member of the family was thinking about leaving.

But sad thoughts do not last forever. Soon Lisa and Matt were laughing and talking. They looked at the road map. They played games and sang songs. They saw farms. They traveled through one town after another.

A Look at Old New England

Late in the morning, they crossed the Connecticut (kə **net** i kət) River. Soon afterward, Mrs. Roberts saw a roadside stand ahead.

"Oh, Ted," she said. "Look at the farmer selling fruits and vegetables. It would be fun to stop and buy some of them. Also, I would like to photograph him and his farm house. That's a part of New England we won't see anymore in a few years."

"What's New England?" asked Matt.

"New England is the name for this part of the country," answered Mr. Roberts. "Today, six states make up New England: Maine, New Hampshire,

A few milk cows graze in the fields of this small New England farm.

Vermont, Massachusetts, Rhode Island, and Connecticut."

Mr. Roberts stopped the car. Everyone got out. They walked over to the tall, white-haired farmer and his stand.

"Mornin'," he said slowly.

Mrs. Roberts looked over the fruits, vegetables, and fresh eggs. She decided to buy a box of blueberries.

"I'd like these," she said. "And, I'd like to take your picture. Your farm will be in the picture, too."

"Go right ahead," the farmer said. "I'm proud of that farm. It's been in my family over two hundred

A farmer's extra vegetables can be sold at a roadside stand.

years. That new barn over there I built with my own hands."

"What do you raise on your farm?" Lisa wanted to know.

"A little of everything," he answered. "Chickens, a few pigs, and cows. Hay to feed the cows. And vegetables to feed us. We grow or make almost all the food we need."

The farmer scratched his head and looked at the red barn.

"It's hard work doing everything yourself. Not much money left over, either," he added. "That's why the children left."

"Your children left this beautiful farm?" Mrs. Roberts asked.

"Yep," he said. "They're grown-up now. They live in the city. Gone south clear to New York City."

"We are going to visit New York City," said Matt.

"Do they ever come back?" Lisa asked.

"Just on vacations," he said. "There is work in the city. Up here, farms can't pay much. And today you need money to buy the things you need. Things you don't raise on farms."

After Mrs. Roberts finished taking pictures, the family drove on. Mr. Roberts talked about the farm they had seen. At one time, most New England farms were like that one. One family grew or made most of

In times past, work horses like these pulled farm wagons and plows.

what they needed. They grew food and made clothes. They built shelters for themselves and their animals. There were no telephones or electric lights. There were no automobiles or running water. A farm family was a small community all by itself.

"Today," Mr. Roberts said, "farming is different. Farms have electric lights. They have running water, cars, and tractors. They have telephones and TV. Roads go from farms to towns and cities."

"In a few more years," Mrs. Roberts said, "farms like that one will be part of our *history* (**his** tər ē)."

Statues help people remember history.

"What's history?" Matt asked.

"You certainly ask hard questions," said his father. "I guess you could say that history is the story of what happened before the present time. Newspaper reporters tell us mostly about the present. People who tell us about the past are called historians."

"I like history," Lisa said. "Last year, we studied the history of the pioneers."

Do You Know?

1. What is the one name for all six northeastern states?
2. What does the farmer raise on his farm?
3. Where does the farmer sell his foods?

Lisa's Log

Lisa decided to keep a log of her trip. A log is like a diary. The log would help her remember the places she saw. It might help her learn to become a reporter.

On the road to
Massachusetts

Monday, August 1

We are going to Plymouth, Massachusetts. Mother says "Plymouth" is an English word. But "Massachusetts" is an Indian word. I have been reading about Plymouth. People who lived there were called Pilgrims. The book says that the Pilgrims were not the first people there. The Pilgrims built their town where Indians had lived. By the time the Pilgrims landed, the Indians were gone. The land was empty. But other Indians lived nearby. They were the Pilgrims' first neighbors.

Which things used by these Indians
come from the *woodlands*?

The First People of the Woodlands

Long ago, the eastern part of our country was covered with forests. There were no roads, farmhouses, or towns. Instead, tall trees covered the land.

Another name for these forests is *woodlands*. Many Indian *tribes*, or groups, once lived in the woodlands. These tribes are sometimes called the Woodland Indians. Indians were the first people to live in our land. They met all their needs from the land.

Look at the map on the next page. A few hundred years ago, forests covered the places where you see

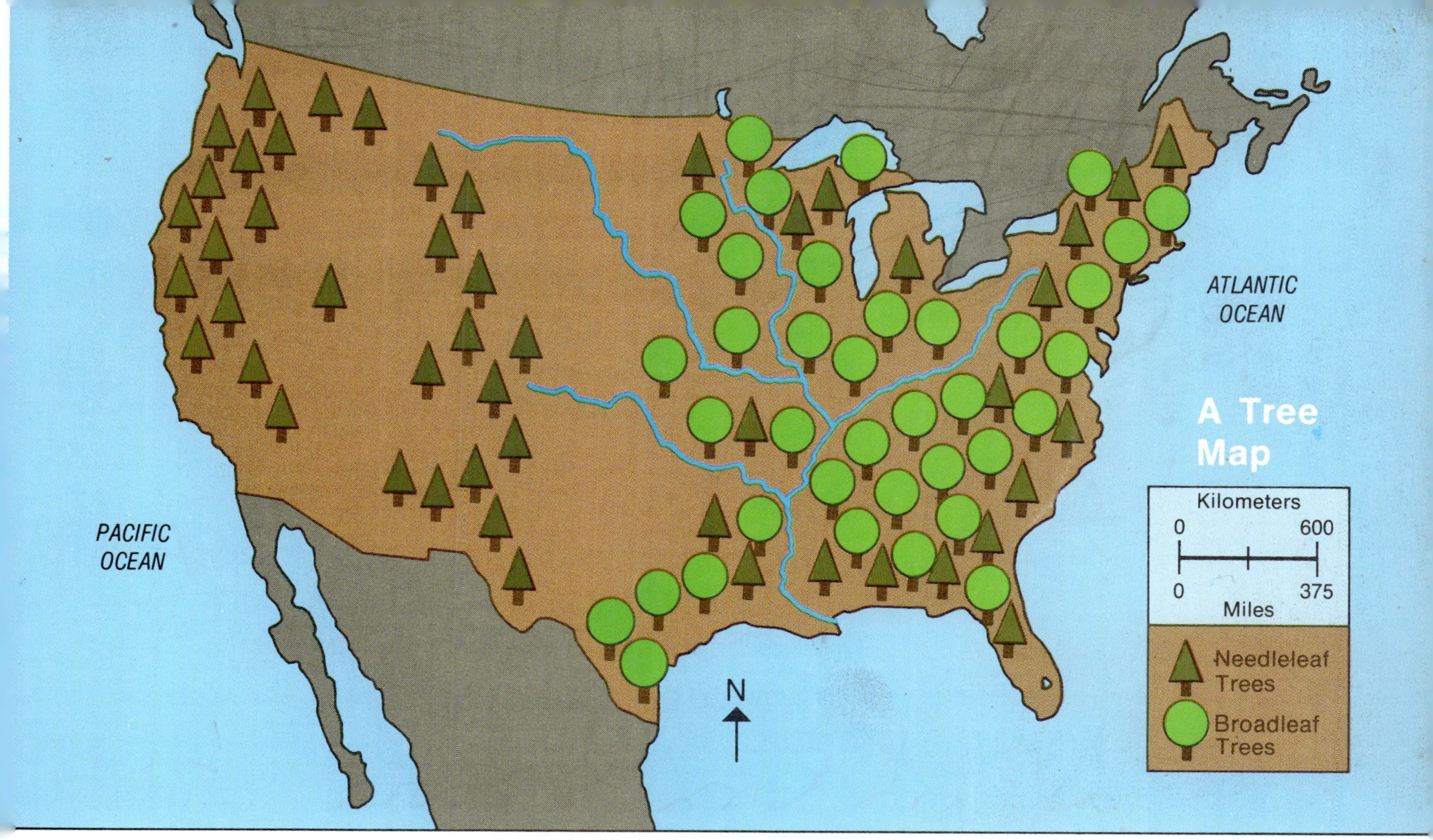

symbols of trees. Compare this map with the rainfall map on page 22. Do trees grow in rainy or dry places?

Getting Food from the Land

The Woodland Indians had many kinds of plants to eat. Some of these plants grew wild. Others were crops. A *crop* is a plant grown to eat or sell.

Sweet, wild strawberries were a summertime treat. In August and September, the Indians picked cranberries and blueberries. Walnuts and chestnuts came from the trees. In spring, they made maple sugar by boiling the sap, or liquid, of maple trees. At the seashore, they were able to find many clams and lobsters.

The Indians cleared the land by cutting and burning trees. Then they could plant crops. In their gardens, the Indians grew beans, squash, pumpkins, and corn.

Corn was a crop discovered by Indians. They planted it in the spring. Into little hills of earth they made holes. Into each hole they dropped three grains of corn. They also put in a small fish for fertilizer (**fûr** ti lī zər). Fertilizer is anything that makes the soil rich so that plants can grow better.

The Indians near Plymouth grew many *crops*. One of them was corn.

By August, a field of tall corn was ready to pick. Some of it they ate. But most of it they dried for winter. They did this by storing it in bark barrels. Sometimes they hung it in bundles in their houses. Today, corn is one of our country's most important crops.

The Indians also cut squash and pumpkins into strips. They dried the strips and stored them in large underground holes lined with skins or bark. These also could last all winter.

The woods were full of animals. Deer, bears, moose, squirrels, and rabbits lived there. The Indians hunted these animals for food. They used some skins for clothing. Other skins were used to cover their houses. Nothing was wasted.

In the forests were many streams, rivers, and lakes. The Indians hunted beaver. They caught fish with bone hooks, nets, spears, and traps. In winter, they cut holes in the ice. They speared fish through the holes.

Do You Know?

1. What are woodlands?
2. What important crop was discovered by Indians?
3. What did Indians do to make sure they had food all winter?
4. What did Indians use animals for?

Above, a *wigwam* is built on a frame. Below, tourists look at a *longhouse.*

Indian Homes

The Indians built their homes from things they found in the woodlands. They made them to suit the weather of each place. Different Indian groups built different kinds of homes.

Most Indian houses were made on frames of wooden poles. The poles were pushed into the ground and bent into different shapes. Then skin, bark, or grass was used to cover the frame.

Some Indian homes were rounded on top. Such homes are called *wigwams* (**wig** wämz). Other houses were *longhouses*. They were divided into rooms. Each family had a room of its own.

Indian Transportation

The way people get from one place to another is called *transportation* (trans pôr **tā** shən). Transportation is also the way people carry things. The Indians had no cars, trains, or trucks. They did not have wheels. What did they do?

First, and most important, Indians used their own feet. They knew how to walk and run quickly and silently. They walked one behind the other. They made paths through the forest. The paths went from one community to another. In winter, they used snowshoes to walk on top of deep snow. In any season, they were able to walk long distances.

Indians often fished from birchbark *canoes.*

Sometimes they had heavy loads to carry. They usually carried these loads on their backs.

For traveling on rivers, the Indians made boats. They made a frame from poles or small trees. Over the frame they stretched animal skins. Or they used the bark from birch trees. These boats are called *canoes* (kə **nōōz**). Some canoes were large enough to hold 20 or more people.

Still other boats were made from logs. The Indians burned these logs at both ends to make them the right length. Then they dug out the inside with sharp stones. Sometimes they burned them out with hot stones. These boats are called *dugouts* (**dug** outs).

Indians often carried sacks like the backpacks that hikers use today.

Today's Indians live differently from
Woodland Indians long ago.

What Happened to the Woodland Indians?

For many years, Indians lived in the woodlands. Animals were important to the way Indians lived. So were trees and plants. When the Pilgrims came, they found friendly Indians to help them. The Indians showed the Pilgrims how to use the things they found around them. The Pilgrims were glad for the help of the Indians. The Pilgrims knew they might not have been able to live without the help the Indians gave them.

But when the Pilgrims arrived, the lives of the Indians changed. Settlers cut down the forests. They built fences, farm houses, and barns. They planted crops on the cleared land. Near the rivers they built dams and mills. There were not as many wild plants and animals as before.

The settlers took over more and more land. The tribes were slowly forced to move away. Over many years, some of them went to new homes in the West. Today, only a few tribes live along the East Coast.

Do You Know?

1. What did Indians use for transportation?
2. What did Indians use to build houses?
3. How did Indians carry big loads?
4. What were two kinds of Indian boats?

A Visit to Plymouth Rock

The Roberts family arrived at the town of Plymouth. Mr. Roberts parked in a lot near the Atlantic Ocean (at **lan** tik ō shən).

Matt and Lisa jumped out. They ran over to where many people stood. They looked at Plymouth Rock.

"Did Pilgrims really land here?" someone in the crowd asked.

"No one knows for sure," said a guide. "But we like to think so. They came ashore somewhere near this spot on December 21, 1620."

The guide was dressed in the clothes of long ago. He wore pants that came to his knees. Long stockings covered his legs between his knees and shoes. Over his jacket he wore a large white collar. He wore a tall hat with a wide brim.

Nearby, the children saw a small wooden ship. It had white sails that were rolled up that day and rope ladders. It was a copy of the ship the Pilgrims used. Even its name, Mayflower, was the same. The Roberts family rowed out and climbed aboard.

"What's a *Pilgrim* (**pil** grim), anyway?" asked Matt.

"Oh, Matt," said Lisa, "You never know anything! Pilgrims are people who make long trips. These Pilgrims came all the way from England years and years ago."

This ship, a copy of the Mayflower, is in Plymouth harbor.

The Trip to the New World

In October 1620, the Mayflower sailed from Plymouth, England. It carried 102 people. Many of them were children. All were going for one reason. They wanted to start a new life in the New World.

The ship did not have an engine as ships do today. It had sails instead. The sails caught the wind. And the wind moved the ship. But sometimes the wind died down. Without it, the ship would stop moving. Other times there were strong winds and big waves. They tossed the tiny ship from side to side.

Too many people lived on one small ship. Families slept together on the floor. Their food was salted beef and dried biscuits. They drank stale water.

While the Mayflower was at sea, a baby was born. His parents named him Oceanus after the Atlantic Ocean. Soon after the Mayflower arrived, a baby girl was born. Her name was Peregrine White.

The *Pilgrims* signed the Mayflower Compact on November 21, 1620.

The *Mayflower Compact*

Two long months passed at sea. Finally, in early winter, the Pilgrims landed. Before they went ashore, they held a meeting. At the meeting, they agreed to make their own laws. And everyone agreed to follow those laws. This agreement became known as the *Mayflower Compact*.

"The Pilgrims were like people in Elmville," said Lisa. "They also make their own laws at town meetings."

Do You Know?

1. What year did the Pilgrims come to Plymouth?
2. How did the Mayflower move without a motor?
3. How long did it take the Mayflower to cross the ocean?
4. What was the name of the Pilgrims' agreement to make and follow their own laws?

Things To Do

1. Find pictures of Indian woodland life.
2. Make a model of an Indian community.
3. Make a class compact similar to the *Mayflower Compact*. Pick the subject of the compact together.

Plimoth Plantation

"We're going to Plimoth Plantation," said Mrs. Roberts. That's the way the Pilgrims spelled Plymouth.

At Plimoth Plantation, Lisa and Matt saw what Plymouth looked like long ago. The houses were not the real ones. They were copies. But they looked exactly as the real ones once did.

The first Pilgrim community was small. The houses were close together. They were made of unpainted wood. Their pointed roofs were made of straw and called thatch (**thach**). The thatch kept out rain. But the roofs often caught fire.

At Plimoth Plantation, you can see how the *Pilgrims* lived.

Windows had no glass. Instead, they were covered with heavy cloth or paper. Fat was rubbed into the panes. In this way, a bit of light could shine through.

Inside the house was a big, open fireplace. It was used for cooking, heating, and light. Some of the rooms seemed almost empty. Most families had only a table, a few chairs, and a bed. Few families had rugs. Those that did, used them to cover tables. The children did not usually have beds. They slept on mattresses filled with corn husks. Older boys and girls slept in an attic called a *loft*.

Pilgrims had no electricity. So they had no electric lights. They made candles for light. They dipped

Plimoth's soldiers sometimes marched to the beat of a drum.

These women are making candles
as the *Pilgrims* did.

several pieces of string into melted wax. Then they hung them on a rack to dry. They dipped them and dried them again and again. After a while, they had a candle.

Warm clothing was needed for cold New England winters. Most Pilgrim women knew how to spin thread or yarn. They made yarn from sheep's wool. They made linen thread from the flax plant. Both yarn and thread were made on a spinning wheel. Then they

A wooden frame keeps the
newly spun yarn straight.

would knit or weave material. Sometimes they mixed linen and wool to make linsey-woolsey. This material was as warm as wool. And it was as strong as linen.

The Pilgrims even made their own soap. First, they let water run through ashes left from burning wood. Then they put the water from the ashes in a big pot. They also put some fat from meat into the pot. After these things had cooked together, they became soap.

Early Trade

The years went by. The Pilgrims learned to meet many of their needs from the land. But they still wanted things from England. To get them, they had to send something in return. So they cut down trees and sawed logs into planks. They trapped beaver for furs. They caught and salted codfish. The salt kept the fish from spoiling. They shipped the planks, furs, and fish to England. In return, they got cloth and furniture. They also got pots and pans. They got shoes, tools, and cattle. They got medicine. This exchange of goods between people is called *trade*.

"Those days seem very far away," said Lisa. "It's hard to think what it was like to live then."

"I'm not sure how I would have liked it," said Mrs. Roberts. "My work would have been very different."

"Let's pretend we're Pilgrims," said Matt.

Do You Know?

1. What did the Pilgrims use for window panes?
2. What did Pilgrims use to make roofs for their houses?
3. What did Pilgrims use to light their houses?
4. What things did the Pilgrims send to England? What did they get back?

A Day in the Life of a Pilgrim Child

Pretend you are a Pilgrim. It is early in the morning. The sun has not yet risen. But it is time for you to get up. Your brothers and sisters also get up.

The girls dress in long, brightly colored dresses. They love red, green, and blue colors. They put on little white caps and aprons. The boys wear bright clothes also. They call dark blue, brown, and green "sad colors." They wear short pants, called knee breeches. In winter, they put on stocking caps.

For breakfast, you eat hasty pudding. Today, hasty pudding is called corn-meal mush. With it, you

This girl, dressed in *Pilgrim* costume, holds a homemade broom.

Pilgrim meals were busy times with many mouths to feed.

may have milk and molasses. There is no tea, coffee, or cocoa in Plymouth.

You eat from a wooden bowl with your fingers. There are no forks in the house. Sometimes you stand. Sometimes you sit on a bench. But, above all, you remain quiet. "Don't speak until spoken to" is a strict Pilgrim rule for children.

After breakfast, the big boys work in the fields. They plow, sow, and reap such crops as corn and beans. In winter, they cut wood and hunt deer and other animals.

This man is thatching a roof at
Plimoth Plantation.

Small boys, like Matt, lead the cows to pasture. They also watch the crops. If they see birds or dogs, they throw stones. The stones scare the birds and animals away. Food must be saved for the people.

Girls like Lisa help their mothers. They stir, or churn, cream to make butter. They help milk the cows and feed the chickens. They clean and wash clothes. They spin to make yarn for clothes. In the outdoor oven, they bake dark bread.

Both girls and boys help thatch the roofs. They both help build houses and dig clams.

You do not go to school. You are too busy to do so. But you have learned to read. Most Pilgrim children use a special kind of book called a *hornbook*. A hornbook is not a book with pages. It is a piece of wood with paper on top. A thin sheet made from the horn of an animal covers the paper. The horn keeps the paper clean. Because there is very little paper, you take good care of it.

Your big meal is in the middle of the day. A favorite dish is succotash (**suk** ə tash). Succotash is a stew of meat, beans, corn, and potatoes. In the evening, you have a light meal. Your father reads aloud from the family Bible. Then he says it is time for bed. You go to bed early and get up early the next day.

Imagine how important this *hornbook* was to a *Pilgrim* child.

Sometimes you stay up late. Then you light a candle. Friends visit and talk over the news of the day.

"What did the children do for fun?" Matt asked.

"Well," said the guide, "children worked. When they weren't working, they were studying. When they weren't studying, they went to church. Not much time was left for games or parties. Now and then there was a wedding party."

"What about Thanksgiving?" asked Lisa.

"Of course," said Mrs. Roberts. "That was their own special day."

Do You Know?

1. When did Pilgrims get up and when did they go to bed?
2. What kind of book did Pilgrim children read?
3. What foods did Pilgrims eat?
4. What work did Pilgrim boys do? What work did Pilgrim girls do?

Things To Do

1. Cut out pictures of things you have that Pilgrim children didn't. Which are basic needs?
2. Trade with a classmate. What will you give and get?

A Special Celebration

Thank the Pilgrims for our Thanksgiving *celebration* (sel ə **brā** shən). A celebration is a special time. It can be a time for remembering. It can be a time for fun. It can be a time for feeling thankful. A birthday party, for example, is to celebrate being born. The Fourth of July is to celebrate the birth of our country. Thanksgiving is our oldest celebration. It took place less than a year after the Pilgrims landed.

The Pilgrims' first winter in New England was hard. At first they had no houses. There was very little food. Many people were sick.

Samoset and Squanto

One day in the early spring, an Indian came to visit. This Indian spoke English. Imagine the Pilgrims' surprise! He said he had learned it from English fishers. He said his name was Samoset (**sam** ō set).

Several days later, he brought a friend to Plymouth. This Indian was named Squanto (**skwon** tō). He, too, spoke English. He taught the Pilgrims Indian ways. The Pilgrims learned to hunt wild animals. They learned to gather fruit and berries. Most important, they learned to grow corn. They learned to meet their needs from the land around them. Squanto lived with the Pilgrims for the rest of his life.

One day, Squanto brought Massasoit (**mas** ə soit) to visit the Pilgrims. Massasoit was the great leader of the Wampanoag (wäm pə **nō** əg) tribe. He did not think of himself as an "Indian." That was a name people from Europe gave his people. He did not think of himself as an "American." There was no word for America then. Massasoit thought of himself as a Wampanoag. That was the name of his tribe, his people. There were, and are today, hundreds of other tribes with other names.

When Chief Massasoit came, he signed a peace treaty with the Pilgrims. He and the Pilgrims agreed not to fight each other. Massasoit stayed friendly with his new neighbors as long as he lived.

Indians taught the *Pilgrims* to grow corn. Here, it is boiled outdoors.

After Squanto taught the Pilgrims how to plant corn, things got better. That summer, the crops grew straight and tall. In the fall, the people gathered the corn. They saw that there was enough to last all winter. No one would go hungry.

Governor William Bradford was the Pilgrims' leader. He wanted to thank God for His goodness. Governor Bradford decided to have a celebration. It would be in the middle of October. First, there would be a church service. Afterwards, there would be a great feast. The Pilgrims would invite their Indian friends. Without them, there would have been no corn for the winter.

After the Thanksgiving feast, the Indians and *Pilgrims* played games.

The First Thanksgiving

Everyone was busy getting ready. The men brought in ducks, geese, and fish. The women baked cornbread. They cooked turnips, onions, beets, and cabbage. For dessert, they would have wild plums and dried berries.

Everyone hoped it would be a fine day. The feast was to be outdoors.

The day finally arrived. Chief Massasoit arrived with 90 people. The Pilgrims wondered how they would feed everyone. The Indians knew what to do. They went hunting and came back with deer meat and wild turkeys.

Before the feast, the people thanked God for His blessings. Then the Pilgrims and Indians sat down outdoors at tables. They ate and ate. Then, both Indians and Pilgrims ran races and wrestled. The Indians won most of the time. The Pilgrims showed them some new games. They taught them how to march in a parade. The Indians had never done that before. They also had fun playing stool ball. Stool ball was played with wooden clubs and leather balls.

The celebration lasted three days. We celebrate Thanksgiving today to remember the first one. Our holiday lasts only one day, and it comes at the end of November. Thanksgiving is an important American holiday.

Today, Americans still give thanks
for their country's riches.

Cranberry Bogs

The next day the Roberts family left Plymouth. They headed for New York City. Along the way, there would be much to see.

"I want you to see a special farm," said Mr. Roberts. "They don't have these farms in New Mexico."

"What's that, Ted?" asked Mrs. Roberts.

"A cranberry farm," said Mr. Roberts.

The cranberry farm had a little train to ride. It had a museum with pictures and farm tools. And it had small *bogs* (**bogz**) where cranberries were grown. A bog is wet, spongy ground. Cranberries grow best in that sort of soil.

The guide explained how cranberries are grown. He said that cranberry vines are planted in sand. During winter, growers flood their bogs. This protects the plants from sudden freezing and warming that might harm them. In late September, the berries are picked. Workers put them in boxes or bags. By Thanksgiving, they are ready to be sold in stores everywhere.

"Are there other kinds of things grown here?" asked Lisa.

"No," said the guide. "Cranberries are the only thing that grows well in these bogs. The farmers grow enough to make a good living. Cranberry farming is big business."

Farmers pick cranberries in time for Thanksgiving Day.

"This farm is different from the one we saw before," said Matt.

"Yes," said Mrs. Roberts. "At the other one, the farmer grew many kinds of things. But there wasn't much left over to sell. Most of it was eaten by his own family. Here, farmers grow a lot of one crop. They grow enough to feed many people. They sell the crop. They make enough money to buy the other things they need."

"And that," said Mr. Roberts, "is what we call specialized (**spesh** ə līzd) farming. Only one special kind of crop is grown."

" 'Specialized' is a hard word," said Matt. "I like the word 'bog' better. I'll think about bogs whenever I eat cranberry sauce."

"I'll think about bogs and specialized farming when I drink cranberry juice next Thanksgiving," said Lisa.

Do You Know?

1. Why was the first Thanksgiving held?
2. Who came to the first Thanksgiving? When was it held?
3. What are cranberry fields called?
4. How is specialized farming different from other kinds of farming?

To Help You Learn

Using New Words

longhouse	wigwam	trade	history
Pilgrim	canoe	crop	tribe

Match each word above with a meaning below.

1. A round top Indian house made of skin or bark
2. An Indian boat made of skin or bark
3. Plants grown in fields or gardens
4. Group of Indians who belong to the same family or live in the same way
5. The story of what happened before the present
6. The exchange of goods between people
7. An Indian house for several families
8. A person who traveled from England to Plymouth on the Mayflower

Mayflower Compact	transportation	dugout
celebration	woodlands	bog
hornbook		

Read each sentence below and put in the missing word. Do not write in this book.

1. Pilgrim children learned to read from a ______.
2. Land covered by forest can be called ______.
3. A ______ is wet, spongy ground.
4. The way people or goods travel is called ______.
5. A ______ is a boat made from a log.
6. The Pilgrims made an agreement called the ______.
7. A ______ is a special time for remembering.

To Help You Learn

Thinking Things Over

1. In what ways did the Indians use things from the land? How did the Pilgrims use them?
2. In what ways was the Pilgrim community of Plymouth like and unlike Elmville?
3. Would you have wanted to be a Pilgrim child in Plymouth? Why? Why not?

Skills: Mapping

Have a mapping lesson at a sand table or box.

1. Make mountains, hills, and level places in the sand.
2. Build a road across the mountains.
3. Make a river come down the side of a mountain.
4. Build a dam across the river. Do you see a lake? Now, draw a map of what you see as you look down.
5. Find a way to show the mountains and hills. How will you be able to tell them apart on your map? (Make them look different from each other.)
6. Draw the road, river, and dam. Make sure that each looks different from the others.
7. At the bottom of your map, make a key to explain how you showed each thing on your map.

UNIT **2**

Cities as Communities

Many people today live in big communities. These are called cities. City people, like the people of Elmville, do not grow their own food. They do not have to make their own clothes. They do not build their own houses. The people in one community need people in another community to help them.

Looking at the Pictures

Can you see how people in a large city get something they need? How else can they get it?

What might the people in a big city make or do that the people of Elmville might need?

Look at the two pictures that show cities. In what ways are the cities alike or different?

Looking Ahead

As you read about these communities, tell:
How are the communities alike?
How are they different from one another?
What is special about each community?

Words to Watch For

Look at the words below. As you read, you will find out what they mean. You will find out how to say them. Look in the Word List, too.

capital	neighborhood
Capitol	plan
government	President
island	skyscrapers

1

One City, Many Communities

"Just look at that!" Mr. Roberts said. "It's worth every extra minute."

"We took the long way to New York City," Mrs. Roberts said. "We came through New Jersey (**jer** zē). That way we could enter New York over the George Washington Bridge."

From the bridge, everyone looked at the view. They were high above the Hudson River. Far in the distance were rose-colored towers. The sun shone on thousands of windows.

Looking at New York City

"Wow! Look at all those buildings," Matt said.

"They are big *apartment* (ə **pärt** mənt) houses, Matt," said Mrs. Roberts. "An apartment house is a building where many families live. Each room or group of rooms is an apartment. Each family makes its home in one apartment. Sometimes tall apartment houses are called 'high rises.' You can see why."

"Why are there so many?" asked Lisa.

"Because there are many, many people in New York City," said Mr. Roberts. "And they all need a place to live."

"More than 7 million people live in New York City," said Mrs. Roberts. "Listen to what this book says. 'More people live in New York City than in all of

Many people live and work in New York. It is a crowded city.

New Mexico and four other states of our country put together.' "

"Just wait until we get downtown," Mr. Roberts said. "Then you'll see even taller buildings. They are so tall they seem to scrape the sky. In fact, they are called *skyscrapers* (**skī** skrā pərz). Look, you can see some of them in the distance. The design they make against the sky is called a *skyline* (**skī** līn)."

"So many New York buildings go up," said Lisa. "Why is that?"

"Good question!" said her father. "This bridge should give you a hint. New York City has many bridges. A bridge, you know, goes over something. The city also has several *tunnels* (**tun** əlz). A tunnel goes underneath the earth's surface."

The Brooklyn Bridge connects one part of New York to another.

The George Washington Bridge is
uptown from the tip of Manhattan.

"I still don't understand," Lisa said.

"This part of New York City is called Manhattan (man **hat** ən)," Mr. Roberts said. "To get here, you must cross a bridge. Or use a tunnel. That's because Manhattan is an *island* (ī lənd). A very small island. On a small island, the only way to grow is *up*, not out.

"An island," Mr. Roberts told them, "is a piece of land that has water all around it. Look at the picture of Manhattan in the guide book. The picture is taken from the air. The tip of the island shows."

Manhattan is the center of New York City. But it is only one part. There are five parts to New York

New York City

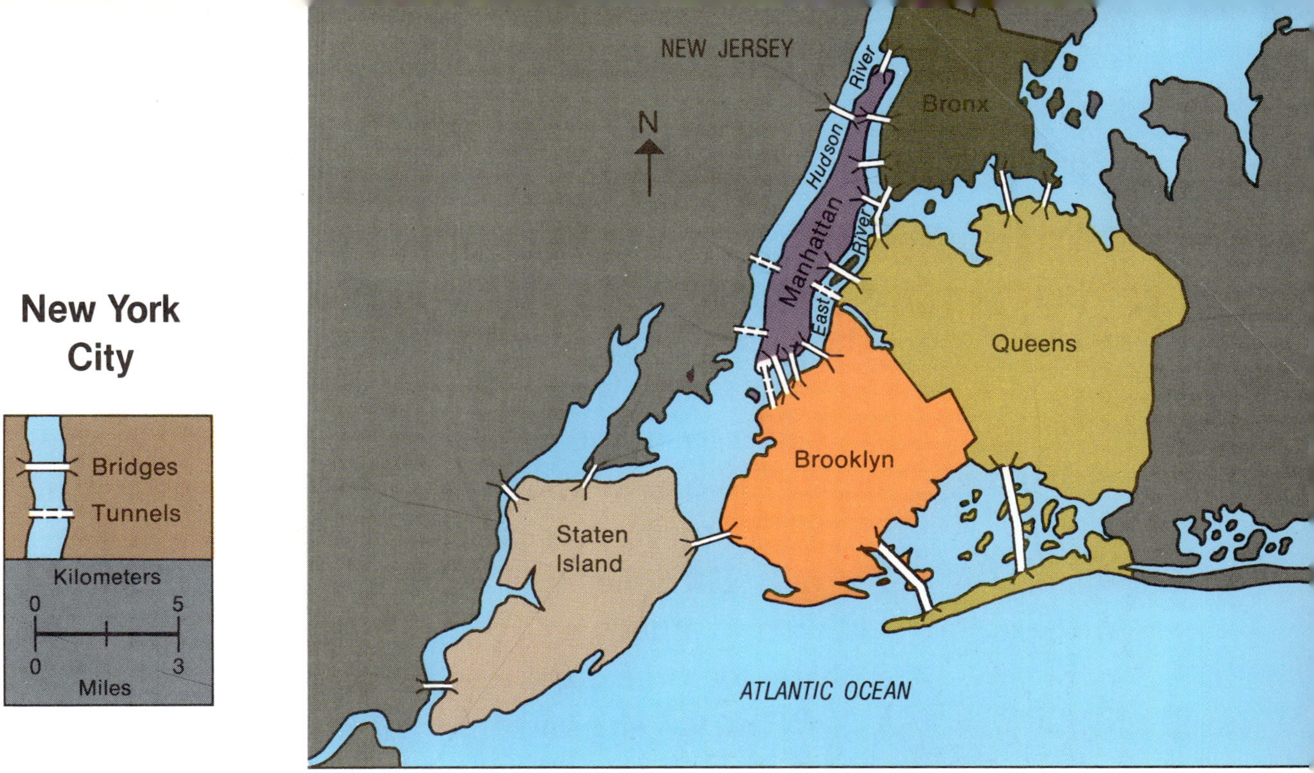

City. Each part is called a *borough* (**bər** ō). Look at the map. What are the five boroughs that make up New York City? Which is biggest? Which is smallest?

Do You Know?

1. What is an apartment house? What other name may some apartment houses have?
2. Why must people use tunnels and bridges to get to Manhattan?
3. Why has New York City grown up instead of out?
4. What are the five parts of New York City called?

Downtown New York

The Roberts family drove into the center of Manhattan. As they drove, the traffic became heavier. The streets became filled with cars, trucks, and buses.

The family went to their hotel. It was in midtown, or the center of the city. They had lunch. Then they decided to see the city. They would start downtown.

Downtown, they parked their car in a garage (gə **räj**). Then they walked down a crowded street. The children kept looking up at the buildings. Mrs. Roberts took the children's hands.

"Hurry," she said. "I want you to see something. I've taken pictures all over this city. But my favorite view is from the top of these buildings."

"Which buildings?" asked Matt.

"The twin towers of the World Trade Center (**wərld trād sen** tər)," she said. "Once the Empire State Building was the tallest skyscraper in New York. It has 102 floors. But now the twin towers are taller. They have 107 floors. Let's go inside and ride to the top."

An elevator (**el** ə vāt ər) zoomed them up. It took only a few seconds. They went up so high, so fast, everybody's ears popped. Then they stepped onto a closed-in deck. There were windows all around.

"I feel dizzy when I look down," Lisa said.

"I'm not surprised," said Mrs. Roberts. "We're over 1,200 feet (400 meters) above the ground."

The twin towers of the World Trade Center rise above other *skyscrapers.*

It was a clear day. Far below, they could see the many narrow streets. On the streets they saw cars and trucks. They saw buses and taxis. From far away, they all looked like bugs. The children could see way uptown. There, they could see the George Washington Bridge. Below them, they looked down on tall buildings all around.

From one window, looking south, they could see New York *harbor* (**här** bər). A harbor is a place of shelter for ships. They could see the Statue of Liberty (**stach** ū **əv** **lib** ər tē). It is on an island in the middle of the harbor. People see it, first thing, as they sail in or out of the harbor.

New York City has one of the biggest and busiest

Visitors can see the Statue of Liberty on a ferryboat ride.

ports (**pôrts**) in the world. A port is a harbor where ships can load and unload goods. Goods from all over the United States arrive at New York's port. Then, they are sent to other countries. Many things coming to the United States from other countries also arrive in New York harbor. Thousands of people work to load and unload the ships that carry the goods.

Lisa looked at the view from each window. Finally she said, "In New York, people and things are always coming and going. I can see all of it by looking around from way up here."

"Not quite," said Mr. Roberts. "There is something you can't see from here. It runs under the ground."

Buildings store goods that are shipped in and out of New York.

People crowd into a *subway* car.
Subways go under the city.

The Subway

The Roberts family rode down to the street. Mrs. Roberts went to get the car. But Mr. Roberts said, "Matt, Lisa, let's take the *subway* (**sub** wā) back to the hotel."

Mr. Roberts led them down many steps. Lisa and Matt found themselves beneath the city streets. They were in a subway station. A subway is a railroad that runs underground. Even here, they walked among crowds of people. They heard a rumble. Two bright lights came out of a dark tunnel. A subway train glided into the station.

The subway train came to a stop. The doors slid open. People poured out of the train. Other people went in. The Roberts family moved inside with the crowd.

"Hold on to this pole," Mr. Roberts shouted. "It will keep you from falling."

All the seats on the train were taken. The children held the pole in the middle of the subway car. The train swayed as it sped through the dark tunnel. Then, suddenly, they were at another station.

"Should we get off?" Matt asked.

"Not yet," Mr. Roberts said. "Our hotel is still a few stops away."

"Are there many stations?" Lisa asked.

"Yes," Mr. Roberts answered. "Subway trains run all over the city. Subways are a big help to New Yorkers. They can carry a lot of people at one time. And they move fast. They don't get caught in the street traffic. Underground trains make sense in a big city."

Do You Know?

1. Why is New York City busy?
2. Name two exciting things about New York City.
3. Why is riding a subway a good way to travel in the city?

Things To Do

1. If you have ridden a subway, tell about it.
2. Cut out pictures of New York City. Put them on the bulletin board.

This *neighborhood* has a park, stores, and apartment houses.

City Neighborhoods

The next morning, the Roberts family took a bus tour. The bus started from midtown Manhattan. First, it went north, to uptown Manhattan.

"Big, big, big! That's the word for New York City!" said Lisa. "Don't New Yorkers feel sort of lonely? How do they get to know each other in such a big city?"

"It's not so hard to make friends here," said Mrs. Roberts. "New York may look like one huge city. But it's really just a lot of *neighborhoods* (**nā** bər hoodz). A neighborhood is a community inside the city. There are more than a hundred neighborhoods in New York City. Other big cities have neighborhoods, too."

A *neighborhood* helps people meet their needs and wants.

"How can I tell one neighborhood from another?" asked Lisa.

"Just keep your eyes open," her mother said. "Each neighborhood has stores and places to eat. It has movies, schools, and places to pray. Look at the signs on the streets. They will tell you something about the neighborhood."

Lisa looked for signs. Soon she saw some. But she could not read them. They were printed in another *language* (**lang** gwij). A language is the way people speak to each other.

"These signs are written in Spanish (**span** ish)," Mr. Roberts said. "Most of the people in this neighborhood are from Puerto Rico (**pwer** tō **rē** kō). In

Puerto Rico, Spanish is spoken. Many Puerto Ricans want to use their language. So they speak it and write it in their own neighborhoods. We say this is a Spanish-speaking neighborhood," Mr. Roberts went on. "It is named after the language of the people. The people here share the same language. Other neighborhoods share other things."

"That's right," Mrs. Roberts said. "In most neighborhoods, people are alike in some ways. They may come from the same country. Or they may speak the same language. Often they have the same way of praying. People move to a neighborhood to be part of a community. They share ways of living. They feel comfortable together."

Many *neighborhoods* have special markets. This one is Italian.

A street fair

"Look," Lisa said. "We are moving into a different neighborhood now. The store signs are written in both Spanish and English."

"Yes," said Mrs. Roberts. "Neighborhoods run into each other."

The bus drove through Harlem (**här** ləm). Harlem is a famous black community. Matt and Lisa saw some big new apartment houses in Harlem. They also saw some very old buildings. Then they went across 125th Street. This street is Harlem's main shopping street. They saw crowded stores and lots of people everywhere they looked.

The bus turned south. It drove down wide avenues (**av** ə no͞oz) and across narrow streets.

Communities have playgrounds where people can meet together.

Chinatown has many places to eat.
Do you see Chinese writing?

"Oh look, children!" said Mrs. Roberts. "Now we're in Chinatown."

There were telephone booths shaped like Chinese buildings. Small shops lined the streets. Many of them had food to serve. Some signs were written in Chinese.

"I've never seen writing like that before," said Matt.

"No," said Mrs. Roberts. "Chinese writing is different from ours. Chinese writing does not have letters. It has signs that stand for words or ideas."

People are growing vegetables in this *neighborhood.*

The bus went on. Lisa saw more signs in different languages. People in New York talk in many languages.

Neighborhoods at Work

In the afternoon, the family went for a walk.

"We're going to see more New York City neighborhoods," Mr. Roberts said. "But this time, they aren't neighborhoods where people live. They are neighborhoods where people work. These places are often called *districts* (**dis** trikts). A district is part of a city, state, or country."

One worker moves racks of finished clothing. Another cuts material.

The family walked to Seventh Avenue in midtown Manhattan. People were rushing in all directions. Some people were pushing racks of clothing on the sidewalks. Many trucks were parked along the street. Many others were on the street.

"What a strange street," Lisa said. "Why in the world are people pushing clothes around on those long clothes racks?"

"We're in the garment (**gar** mənt) district," said Mrs. Roberts. "A garment is a piece of clothing. This is where clothes are made. People all over our country wear clothes made here. The garment business is a big business in New York.

On Wall Street you see banks, office buildings, and even hot dog stands.

"Thousands and thousands of people work right here in the garment district. Workers move the racks of clothing from buildings to trucks. The trucks carry the clothing to other places. This is one of the busiest streets in the city."

Lisa and Matt saw other work districts. They walked along Fifth Avenue and saw many shops. They rode the subway again to Wall Street. They walked along Wall Street, the center of the financial (fī **nan** shəl) district. Financial means having to do with money matters. Here, they saw many banks and office buildings. These places do business all over the country.

TOMORROW'S
Weather
CLOUDY
COOLER
HOTEL ASHLEY
THE BOWERY
EVERYBODY
LOVES
ANNIE
A New Musical
ALVIN THEATRE
250 West 52nd Street
PALACE
entrance
Tareyton lights

"Next, we will go to my favorite part of New York City," said Mrs. Roberts.

When they got there, Mrs. Roberts said, "This is called the theater (**thē** ə tər) district. Most people call this area Broadway (**brôd** wā). The streets with theaters are off the main avenue, Broadway. This is where you can see the latest plays and musical shows. This is where you can see famous actors and actresses."

"Oooh, look! I think I see one now!" said Lisa. A shiny black car drove quickly by.

"Who? Who?" asked Matt.

"I don't know," said Lisa, a little sadly. "The car went by too fast."

"Never mind," said their father. "We've saved the best for last. Let's go to Central Park."

Do You Know?

1. What is a neighborhood?
2. Why do people come together in neighborhoods?
3. What are two work districts of New York City?

Things To Do

1. On a map of your community, circle your neighborhood.
2. Draw a picture of your home. What kind of building is it? An apartment, or a house?

Taxis wait for people coming out of an afternoon show on Broadway.

In Central Park

Lisa and Matt were tired, but happy. They had seen all the animals in the zoo. Now they were ordering hot dogs. The man selling hot dogs had a little stand on the sidewalk.

"Would you like a treat?" asked Mrs. Roberts.

"Oh, yes please," said Matt.

"What do you want on your hot dog?" the man asked Matt.

"Everything!" Matt said.

The man piled pickles, onions, mustard, and sauerkraut on the hot dog. Matt tasted it. It was wonderful.

Central Park brings trees and open space into the crowded city.

"I like Central Park best of all," Lisa said. "It's such a surprise. One minute, you see just skyscrapers. The next minute, you see trees and grass."

"Yes," said Mrs. Roberts. "This is one of the biggest and oldest parks in our country. The people who planned it thought parks were important. They believed that everybody needs to enjoy nature. We know they were right. People need to have a place to relax. They need to have a place to play games."

The family saw one boy carrying a model sailboat.

"Where can he sail that?" Matt asked.

"In a place called Sailboat Pond," said Mrs. Roberts.

Eating, playing, and relaxing are all fun in Central Park.

"Can big boats sail there, too?" asked Matt.

"Not on the pond," said Mrs. Roberts. "But there is a lake in the park. People may rent rowboats. Central Park also has playgrounds, an ice-skating rink, and tennis courts."

"I thought the zoo was the most fun of all," said Lisa. "I loved the monkeys."

"I thought the elephants were best!" said Matt.

The next morning, the Roberts family got ready to leave New York. Lisa and Matt were thinking about the city.

"There are a lot of people in this city," said Matt. "It is very big."

"I liked the different neighborhoods," said Lisa. "People here live, and work, in so many different ways."

"I wish we could have gone to the theater," put in Mrs. Roberts. "New York is famous for its plays, dance companies, music. People come from all over to take part in these cultural (**kul** chər əl) activities."

"New York is like many other cities," said Mr. Roberts. "It is big. There are many people. There is a lot going on. But it is also special. It is important to our whole country. It is a financial center. It is a cultural center. It is a center for business."

"Someday, I'd like to come back here," said Lisa. "I'd like to stay in one of those high rises. Way up high."

This view is of midtown Manhattan.
It shows you how big the city is.

Los Angeles: A Major City on the West Coast

Los Angeles, like New York City, is a large city near an ocean. But there are differences between the two cities.

Look at the buildings. How are they different from buildings in New York City?

Look at the trees. How are they different from trees in Central Park?

What other differences do these pictures show?

CASA CAROLINA
W-21

New Jersey Truck Farming

The family left Manhattan through the Lincoln Tunnel. They were going south to Washington. They would drive through New Jersey. As they drove they saw many communities.

"These communities are *suburbs* (**sub** ərbz)," said Mr. Roberts. "A suburb is a place to live on the edges of a city. Most people in the suburbs work in a city. Many people here travel in and out of New York City every day."

The Roberts saw many parts of New Jersey as they went. New Jersey is a state where many goods are made. It also grows many vegetables.

This is a *community* in the *suburbs.*
Where do most of the people work?

The family saw trucks going north towards New York City. They were loaded with crates, or boxes, of fresh vegetables.

"Look at all that corn!" said Matt.

"And all those tomatoes!" said Lisa.

"People in New York City need a lot of vegetables," said Mrs. Roberts. "That's why the trucks are carrying them."

"Where do the vegetables come from?" Lisa asked.

"Probably from a *truck farm* (**truk farm**) here in New Jersey," Mr. Roberts said. "The soil here is good for growing vegetables. The land is flat and there is enough rainfall."

Many trucks are on the highways between New Jersey and New York.

"Are they called truck farms because the vegetables are sent in trucks?" Lisa asked.

"That would make sense," Mr. Roberts said with a laugh. "But that's not the reason. A long time ago, farmers brought their vegetables to town to *barter* (**bär** tər). Barter means to trade without using money. Another word for barter was 'truck.' As time passed, people started to call vegetables 'truck.' So, truck farming came to mean growing and selling vegetables."

"May we visit a truck farm?" Lisa asked.

"Yes, let's do that," said Mr. Roberts.

The truck farm was large. The family saw vegetables growing in long, straight rows. They saw tomatoes, asparagus, lettuce, peppers, potatoes, and sweet corn. Stacks of crates stood ready to be filled with vegetables. There were sheds where workers

Crates of corn from this *truck farm* will be sent to New York City.

packed the vegetables for shipping. The family talked to the farmer in charge.

"This is a lot of food," Mr. Roberts said. "How do you manage to grow so much?"

"I have help," said the farmer. "I have many people to help me. But I also have machines to help. They help turn the soil. They plant the seeds. And they help gather the crops. These machines are more powerful than the tools of long ago."

"I know," Lisa said. "The Pilgrims had only a few simple tools. They had hoes and rakes. They had to push their own plows. Later, a few lucky people had horses to pull the plows. But farming was hard work."

"Farming with machines is hard work, too," the farmer said. "But we can grow much more food today than the Pilgrims could."

Machines help with plowing, but workers pick tomatoes by hand.

Machines help workers sort and
pack tomatoes faster.

Lisa thought about the New England farmer they had met. His farm had been very small. This truck farm was big. It takes many big farms to feed everybody in New York City.

"Your land looks like a great, big vegetable garden," Matt said.

The farmer smiled and said, "Maybe that's why we call New Jersey the Garden State."

Do You Know?

1. Name some things people can do in Central Park.
2. Which state has many truck farms that send vegetables to New York City?
3. How did truck farms get their name?
4. How are modern farm tools different from Pilgrim tools?

Using New Words

To Help You Learn

apartment	island	port
skyscraper	neighborhood	tunnels
skyline	district	language
borough	harbor	barter
suburbs	subway	truck farm

Read the words listed above. Which ones do you think tell most about New York City?

Choose the six words that you think best describe New York City. Then use each one in a sentence.

Write a sentence using each word left over.

Talking It Over

1. How are the high rise apartment buildings in New York City like the family houses in Elmville? How are they different? Which is more like your home?
2. Are there neighborhoods of different people in your community? Do they help make a city interesting?
3. How are harbors and ports alike? How are they different? Which is more important for transportation?
4. Why is transportation important to people who live in New York City and the suburbs?

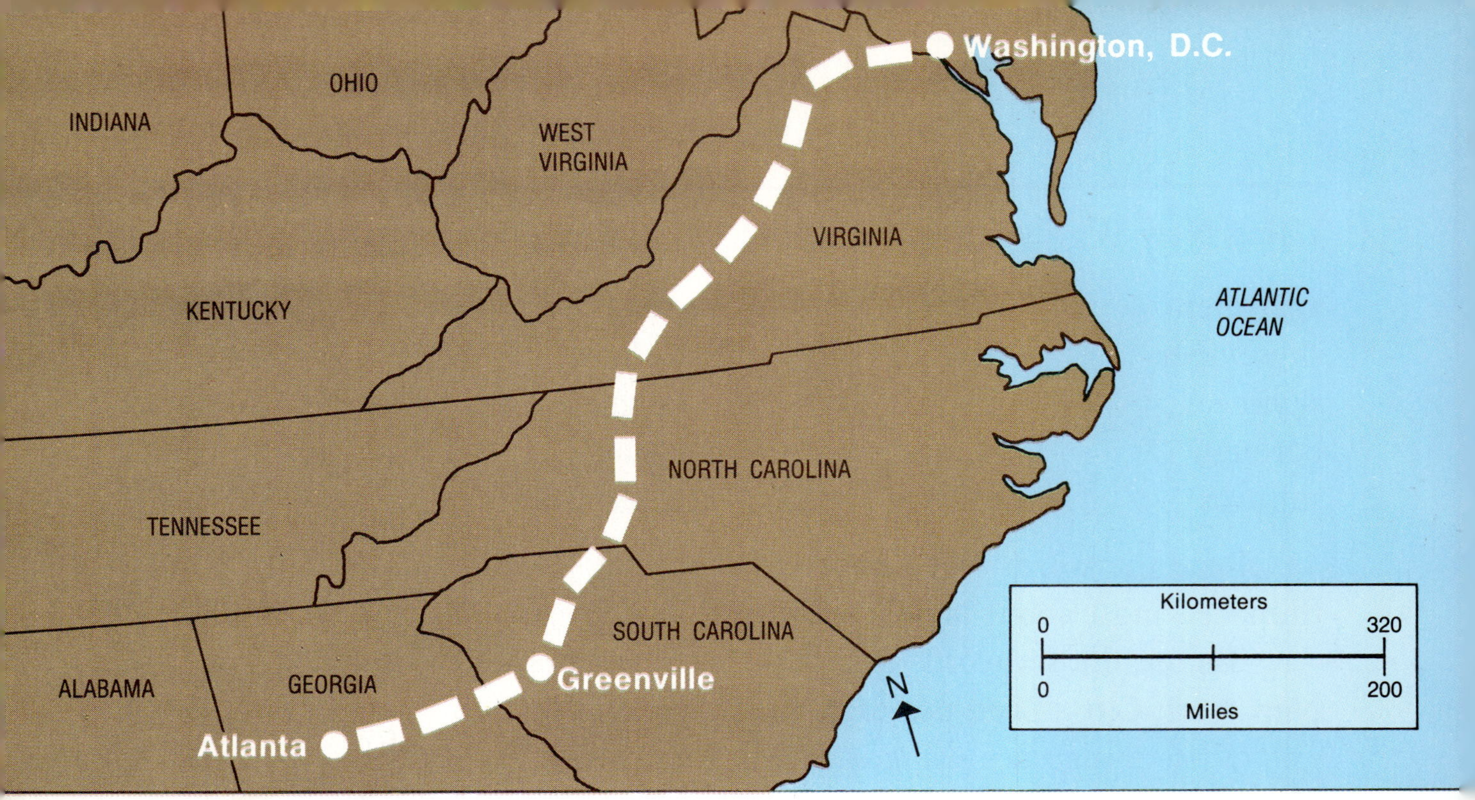

2

Our Nation's Capital

The road sign showed that the Robertses were close to Washington (**wäsh** ing tən). Yet they saw no skyline such as in New York City. The car was hot and stuffy. Lisa began to wriggle in her seat.

"It can't be much of a city without skyscrapers," she said. "I don't think Washington is so special."

"That's not so," said Mrs. Roberts. "It is a very special city. Sit up and listen to something."

Mrs. Roberts read from a book about Washington.

The Capitol Is Not the Capital

Washington, D.C., is our country's *capital* (**kap** ə təl) city. Our leaders meet and work in the capital. That is where they make our laws. That is where they run the country's business.

The main building where our leaders meet also has a name. It is called the *Capitol* (**kap** ə təl). The word for the building sounds like the word for the city. But it is spelled differently. Look at both words. How are they different?

The Capitol is a very important building in Washington. Our early leaders wanted people to see it easily. So they made a law. It says that no building in Washington can be higher than the Capitol. That is why Washington has no tall buildings.

The *Capitol* can be seen from many directions in Washington, D.C.

One of Washington's newest buildings
is the Air and Space Museum.

Washington is also special in another way. It is a city without a state. Elmville, you remember, is in the state of Vermont. New York City is in New York State. Washington, D.C., is between two states, Maryland and Virginia. But it does not belong to either one.

Washington belongs to the whole country. The part that belongs to the whole country has a name. It is called a *federal* (**fed** ə rəl) *district*. "Federal" means "of our country."

"Very often, the word Washington also has the letters D.C. after it. They stand for *District of Columbia*," Mr. Roberts said. "Can anybody guess why the federal district is named Columbia?"

Both Lisa and Matt thought. But they had no idea. Mr. Roberts laughed.

"Here's a hint. Who discovered America?" Mr. Roberts asked.

"Columbus," the children shouted.

"Right! So why is the federal district named the District of Columbia?"

"After Columbus," they said.

"Washington," said Mrs. Roberts, "is named after our first President (**prez** ə dənt). George Washington helped pick out the place where the city would be built. He helped to plan the city. He laid the first stone for the Capitol building. But he never saw even one building finished. And he was shy about calling the city 'Washington.' He always said 'Federal City' instead."

Do You Know?

1. What is a capital?
2. What is the Capitol?
3. What does D.C. stand for?
4. What did George Washington call the capital?

City Tour

Lisa and Matt got up early the next morning. The Robertses stayed in a motel. A motel is a place for people to sleep. By eight o'clock, the family was on its way. They planned to see Washington before the day became hot.

They drove down wide streets. The streets were lined with trees. In some places the streets were not straight. They were circles. In the middle of the circles were statues (**stach** ūz) and fountains (**foun** tənz). Large, white buildings lined the streets. Little parks were everywhere.

Suddenly Lisa shouted.

"Oh, wow! Look! Look what I see!"

Many Americans visit the White House every year.

Everyone turned. There was the White House. The White House is where the *President* and the President's family live. The President is our main *elected* (i **lekt** əd), or chosen, leader. The President, and the President's helpers, work together in the same building.

Then Matt shouted even louder.

"Look! Look what I see! Over there!" He pointed to a tall, white stone tower. Around the base of the tower was a circle of American flags.

"It's the Washington Monument (**mon** yə mənt)," said Mrs. Roberts.

"Mon-u-ment," Matt repeated, slowly. His mother laughed.

On the Fourth of July, you can see fireworks over the Potomac River.

"Oh, Matt," she said. "I just remembered. When I was a little girl, I always said 'mommyment' instead of 'monument.' I thought the word had something to do with mothers. But a monument is really something put up to remember a person. Or, it is put up for remembering something that happened. This great monument helps us remember George Washington."

"See that!" Mr. Roberts said suddenly. "There's the Lincoln Memorial (**ling** kən mə **môr** ē əl). A memorial is another way of remembering somebody or something. Let's stop the car and take a look."

The Lincoln Memorial

Mrs. Roberts parked the car. The family climbed many steps. They walked higher and higher. Inside, the building was dark and cool. The children looked up at a huge statue. They saw the face of President Abraham Lincoln.

Mrs. Roberts put her arms around both children. Together, they looked at the statue.

"President Lincoln kept our country together," she whispered. "Long ago, people in the North and people in the South fought a war. The South wanted to break away from the United States. The southern leaders wanted to form their own country. But President Lincoln kept the country together."

"Like we're staying together," said Matt, "by going to New Mexico with Daddy."

Most visitors stop to look at this famous statue of Abraham Lincoln.

"We remember Lincoln for another reason," said Mr. Roberts. "Before Lincoln was President, most black people in our country were slaves. They could not work or live where they wanted. But Lincoln changed that. He decided they should be free."

"This city, and President Lincoln, are very important to all Americans," said Mrs. Roberts. "But black Americans have a special feeling for Lincoln and this city. Many blacks live here in Washington."

"Yes," said Mr. Roberts. "They have always played an important part in our capital's history. A black man, Benjamin Banneker (**ben** jə mən **ban** ə kər), helped build Washington."

Benjamin Banneker used this tool to measure our *capital's* land.

Mrs. Roberts took photos of the statue. Then the family turned to leave. At the top of the stairs they stopped. Before their eyes was a wonderful sight. They saw a long, grassy park. Halfway down the park stood the Washington Monument. At the end of the park was the Capitol. It sparkled in the morning sun.

"Gee!" said Lisa. "What a great view! Why did I say Washington was not special? It's the most beautiful city I've ever seen!"

"Washington is beautiful," said Mr. Roberts. "A lot of other cities just grew. People didn't think about how they looked. But Washington is different. Our early leaders wanted a new city as the capital. So they began to *plan* (**plan**) their new capital. A plan is something that has been worked out ahead of time. Washington is a planned city.

Do You Know?

1. What is the President's house and office called?
2. How did President Lincoln help our country?
3. How is our capital different from most other cities?

Things To Do

1. Tell your class about cities you have lived in or visited. Point them out on the classroom map.
2. List famous places or buildings in your community.

A Planned City

Our early leaders decided they wanted a new capital. They wanted a new town for their new *government* (**guv** ərn mənt). Government is all the people who make the laws and run the country. But choosing a place for a government town was not easy. People in the South wanted the city in the South. People in the North wanted the city in the North. Finally in 1790, they agreed what to do. The capital would be built along the Potomac (pə **tō** mək) River. This river was right between the North and the South.

The leaders asked President Washington to choose the best spot. He knew this part of the country well.

George Washington lived at Mount Vernon as a farmer for many years.

His own farm, Mount Vernon (**mount vər** nən), was also on the Potomac River.

People from all over the country would want to visit the capital. So would people from across the ocean. Finally, Washington found a spot near a main road and where ships could dock.

The Planner of Our Capital

A French engineer named Pierre L'Enfant (pē **er** lon **fon**) asked to help plan the capital. L'Enfant was helped by Benjamin Banneker and Andrew Ellicott (**an** dro͞o **el** ə kət). These men found out how much land there was. They drew the map as L'Enfant wanted it.

George Washington is known as the Father of Our Country.

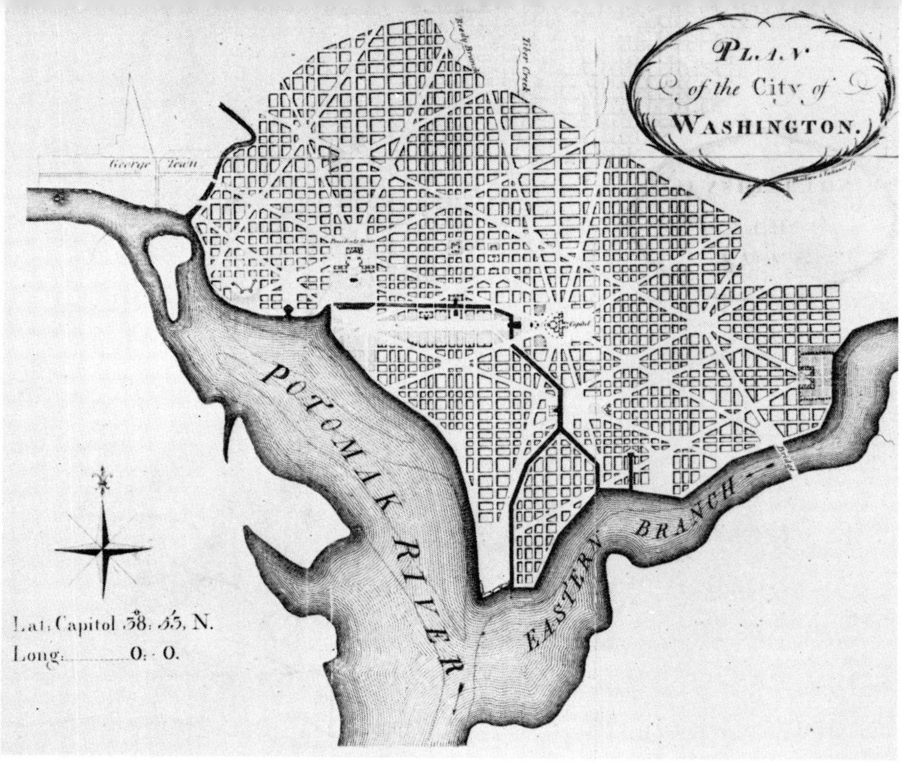

L'Enfant's *plan* for Washington, D.C., was drawn by Ellicott and Banneker.

L'Enfant knew the Capitol building would be important. He thought it should be like the center of a wheel. On the map, Ellicott and Banneker drew the Capitol. They put it in the center of the town. They drew streets going out from the Capitol. Those streets look like the spokes of a bicycle wheel. L'Enfant planned a wide, grassy park from the Capitol to the river. He wanted a place for people to walk and enjoy themselves.

L'Enfant knew the capital would need many streets. He knew they should be easy to remember. So he planned streets running north and south. He gave

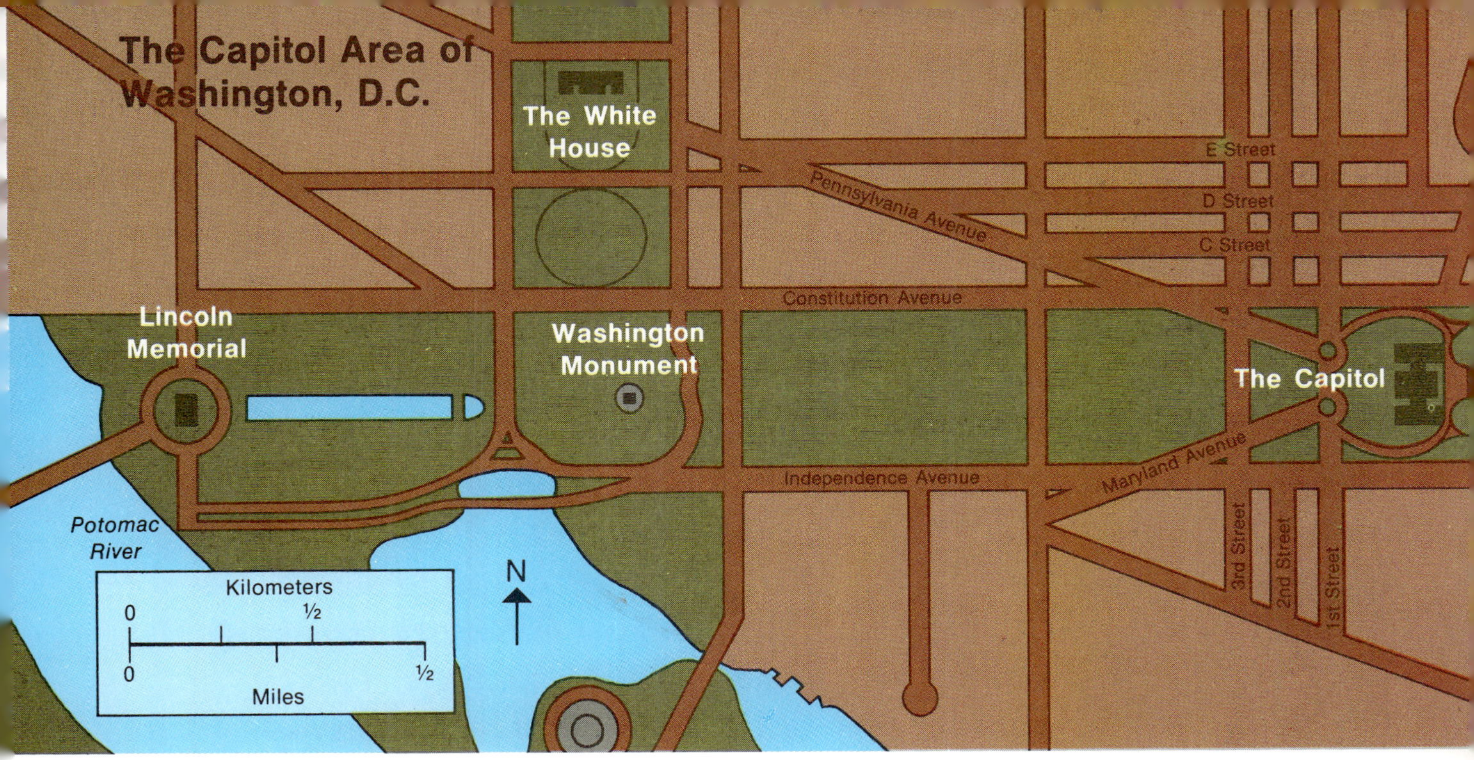

them numbers for names. (Look at the map.) L'Enfant also planned streets running east and west. He named them after letters of the alphabet. (Look at the map again. You'll see, there are no "A" and "B" streets. Those streets have other names.)

Pierre L'Enfant never saw his plans come true. He quarreled with some of the city leaders. He left, taking the plans with him.

For years, no more work was done. Then, after a long time, building started again. Benjamin Banneker remembered the plans. He put the plans together again, using almost all of L'Enfant's ideas.

The *Capitol* dome

A Visit to the Capitol

The next day, the Roberts family again got up early. They drove past the White House once more. Soon they arrived at the Capitol building. They parked the car. The family crossed the street and entered a large office building. They took the elevator and walked down the hall. Over one door was a sign. It said "Charles Alvarez, New Mexico."

"Who is Charles Alvarez?" asked Lisa.

"Mr. Alvarez is a *member of Congress* (**kong** rəs) from our new home," said Mrs. Roberts. That means he was elected to be one of our country's leaders. He helps to make the laws. He helps decide what things our country will do."

"How many members of Congress are there?" asked Lisa.

"Good heavens, Lisa," said her mother. "Daddy and I don't know everything! Ask Mr. Alvarez. We have a meeting with him now."

Meeting a Member of Congress

Inside, a young man led them into Mr. Alvarez's office. Mr. Alvarez shook hands with Mr. and Mrs. Roberts. Then he shook hands with Matt and Lisa. Lisa had never felt such a strong handshake before. She smiled. Mr. Alvarez gave her a big smile back.

"So you are moving to the Sunshine State," he said.

In this room visitors can watch
Congress at work.

"Is that what you call New Mexico?" Lisa asked shyly.

"It certainly is," he said. "And sunshine is what we've got. But that's not all. We've got mountains. We've got flatlands. We've got wild animals. We've got sheep and cows. We've got cowboys. We've got Indians. We've got *Hispanic* (his **pan** ik) *Americans*.

"What's a Hispanic American?" asked Matt.

Mr. Alvarez smiled again.

"You're looking at one, Matt," he said. "Some of us came from Mexico (**mex** i kō). Most of the pioneers who came to the Northeast came from England. Most of the pioneers who came to the Southwest came from Mexico or Spain.

"My family came to New Mexico before the Pilgrims landed at Plymouth," Mr. Alvarez went on. "New Mexico was part of Spain, then. Next, it was part of Mexico. Now, it is part of the United States. A lot of people there speak Spanish."

"Is it hard to learn?" asked Lisa.

"Not very hard," said Mr. Alvarez. "Maybe you'll study Spanish in school. Maybe you'll learn to eat some Mexican food, too. I bet I know one Mexican food you eat."

"What's that?" asked Lisa.

"Chili (**chil** ē)," said Mr. Alvarez.

"We love chili," said Matt.

A *page* can be a big help to a busy *member of Congress.*

"That's great," said Mr. Alvarez. "But you had better start putting in more chili pepper. We like our food hot. Spicy hot!"

Then Mr. Alvarez turned to Mr. and Mrs. Roberts. He talked to them about the new dam. He told them that Congress had studied the plans. He said that scientists had studied the plans also. No one wanted to harm the plants and animals near the dam.

"Things look good," said Mr. Alvarez. "It looks as if you can go ahead with your plans."

He sat and thought for a minute.

"You know what?" he added. "That dam is going to bring a lot more people to the desert. You wait and see. People love sunshine. I hope they will like me well enough to send me back to Washington. Then I can keep on working for them here in Congress."

"What kinds of things do you do?" Lisa asked.

"Anything and everything," said Mr. Alvarez. "I help make laws which help the country. I help make laws to help New Mexico. I read the letters people write. I try to do most of the things they ask. But I can't do what everyone wants all the time. People sometimes disagree on what makes a good law. Then I write letters back home. I tell people what I've done. I go to meetings. A lot of meetings. Sometimes I talk to big groups of people. And I meet people who come to Washington. People like you. That's important."

"It sounds like a lot of work," said Lisa. "How do you get it all done?"

"Members of Congress have a lot of helpers," Mr. Alvarez said. "The people here in my office help me with my work."

"Oh, your work sounds interesting," Lisa said.

"You know who else helps, Lisa?" asked Mr. Alvarez. "*Pages* (**pā** jəz) do. Pages are boys and girls 14 to 18 years old. They help out when Congress meets. They do all sorts of jobs. One job is to run errands. Congress couldn't get along without them."

Lisa's eyes lit up. It would be exciting to be a page, she thought. She would like that.

Pages help mail packages and letters.

The Roberts family got up to leave. Mr. Alvarez shook hands all around again.

"Goodbye," he said. "Adios (ad ē **os**)."

"Adios," said Matt and Lisa.

"Now you know some Spanish," said Mrs. Roberts.

After leaving, Lisa suddenly remembered something. She ran back into the office.

"Excuse me, Mr. Alvarez," she said. "Can you tell me one thing more. How many members of Congress are there?"

"Of course," he said. "There are 535 members of Congress. Don't forget that, Lisa."

"I won't," said Lisa, waving goodbye. "I'm going to be a page someday."

Do You Know?

1. Who decided where to build the capital?
2. Who planned our capital city?
3. What sort of things do members of Congress do?

Things To Do

1. Make a list of big cities between New York and Washington. Put them on your outline map.
2. Trace the Robertses' route on your map.

In the Mountains

The Roberts family said goodbye to Washington, D.C. They drove south into the mountains. The mountain air was fresh and cool. It was a nice change to look at trees instead of buildings.

To pass the time, everyone talked about the mountains. Lisa and Matt learned that our country has two main groups of mountains. They used a map to find out where they are. Look at the mountain map on this page. What are the mountains in the West called? These mountains are very high. Now look for the Appalachian (a pe **lā** chē ən) Mountains. Where are

A Mountain Map

they found? These are the mountains Lisa and Matt saw. They are not as high as our western mountains.

Gone Fishing

The Robertses' first night in the mountains was exciting. It rained hard. The raindrops sounded like a drum beating. And the wind howled like a wild animal. At first, Lisa and Matt were scared. Then Mr. Roberts explained the sound. He said that wind often makes strange noises in the mountains. It sweeps through narrow valleys. It roars down mountain slopes.

By the next morning, the storm had passed. Lisa

Trout fishing in cold mountain *streams* is a popular sport.

went fishing with her father in a mountain *stream* (**strēm**). Lisa took off her shoes and went wading.

"Oooh, it's cold!" she squealed.

"Mountain streams are always cold," said her father. "Clear and cold." He cast his line into the water. "Let's just hope this one is full of fish."

"Why does the stream run so fast?" she asked.

"Because it's coming downhill," said her father. "First it rains on the mountains, as it did last night. Then the rain runs quickly down in little streams. As they run, the streams join each other. They become larger streams. At the bottom of the mountain, they start to run slower. Streams from one mountain may join streams from another mountain. After many streams have come together, they make a river."

"Then, a river is just a lot of little streams that got together," said Lisa.

"That's right," said Mr. Roberts.

Suddenly he felt a tug on his line. He reeled it in. He took the fish and held it up for Lisa to see. It was a big trout.

A Textile Mill

The Robertses stopped for a while in Greenville, South Carolina (ka rə **lī** nə). It was their last stop before Atlanta.

"Remember when we visited the garment district?" Mrs. Roberts said.

Lisa's Log

Great Smoky Mountains
Monday, August 15

Today we stopped at a craft center. A craft center is a place where the mountain people make and sell things. Mother took pictures.

I saw a woman making a bed cover. She sewed little pieces of cloth together. She made the pieces into a pretty picture.

I saw a man working with wood. He said he was making a "dulcimer." He played a song on one he had finished. I loved the music.

I spoke to a girl my age. Her name was Nellie Jo. She was making dolls out of corn husks. She said she lived in a cabin down in the hollow. That means in the valley between the mountains. She said her Dad works in the sawmill. He saws up logs to make boards.

These big, powerful looms can
produce large amounts of cloth.

"Way back in New York?" asked Matt.

"Yes. Remember, you asked where they made the cloth. Well, this is where a lot of the cloth comes from."

Mrs. Roberts pulled the car up to a large, brick building.

"We are going to visit a *textile mill* (**tek** stīl **mil**)," she said. A textile mill is a place where thread is made into cloth. "Textile" is another word for cloth.

Inside the building, many people were working. They ran large, noisy machines. One of the women came over to meet the family.

"In the old days," she said, "cloth was made by hand. People used a tool called a hand loom. Today, most cloth is made on power looms run by electricity (i lek **tris** ət ē). We can make a lot more cloth that way. And it takes much less time."

"What sorts of cloth do you make?" Mr. Roberts asked.

"We make a lot of cotton cloth," said the woman. "Farmers in the South used to grow all the cotton. Now, farmers in the Southwest grow more cotton. We make this cotton into cloth.

"The cloth comes out of the machines on rolls. We load the rolls onto trucks. And the trucks carry the cloth to New York City. There, it is made into clothes. Other cities make clothes, too. The new clothes are loaded onto trucks again. And some of them come right back here to be sold in department stores.

"Look at this dress. We made the cloth here in Greenville. People in New York City cut it and sewed it. And I bought the dress from a store around the corner, here in South Carolina."

Mr. Roberts smiled at the woman and said, "That's what I'd call a well-traveled dress."

Do You Know?

1. What are the two main groups of mountains in our country?
2. Where does rain on a mountain go?
3. What is a craft center?
4. What do you call a place where thread is made into cloth?

To Help You Learn

Using New Words

District of Columbia	capital	elected
Hispanic American	Capitol	government
member of Congress		

Read each sentence below and put in the missing word. Do not write in this book.

1. A _____ speaks Spanish.
2. An _____ leader is a chosen leader.
3. The _____ is a building in Washington.
4. The _____ is named for Columbus.
5. A _____ is an elected leader.
6. A _____ city is where our laws are made.
7. _____ is all the people who run the country.

federal district	President	plan
planned city	streams	page
textile mill		

Match each word from the list above with one of the meanings below.

1. Many of these make a river
2. Where thread is made into cloth
3. Our main elected leader
4. A city that was planned ahead of time
5. Something that has been worked out ahead of time
6. A boy or girl who helps out in Congress
7. A place that belongs to the whole country

To Help You Learn

Talking It Over

1. In what ways is Washington, D.C., a special city? How is it different from New York City?
2. How is the town meeting in Elmville like Congress in Washington? How is it different?
3. Why does a country need laws? Why does it need a government?
4. What are the differences between a planned city and a city that just grew? In which kind of city would you rather live? Why?

Activities: Studying History

What do you know about the history of your own community? Gather more facts by talking to someone who knows a lot about it.

Write to invite that person to visit.

Think about what you want to find out.

How did your community get its name? How did your community begin? Who were the first people to live there? Make a list of questions.

Write down the answers your guest gives.

If you can, find out more facts. Ask the librarian in your school or community to help you. Try to find some pictures of your community in the past.

UNIT **3**

Communities at Work

Communities may be different from each other. But they are alike in one important way. In all communities, people work to get what they need. In this part of the book, you will read about communities at work.

Looking at the Pictures

Look at the people working in these pictures. Do people in your community do any things you see here?

What other jobs do people in your community have? How do they help people meet their needs?

As you read this part of the book, try to find out in which community each picture was taken. What things in the picture help you tell?

Looking Ahead

How would each community be different if it were in another place?

How do communities help each other?

How do different people help make their community interesting?

Words to Watch For

Look at the words below. As you read, you will find out what they mean. You will find out how to say them. Look in the Word List, too.

border	crossroads	gulf	orchard
coast	fuel	levee	transportation center

1

Crossroads of the Southeast

"Dad, are we almost at Great-Aunt Kate's house?" Matt asked.

"We're almost there," Mr. Roberts answered.

The Roberts family had been traveling all day. They were planning to visit their Great-Aunt Kate. She had lived in Atlanta all her life.

"I'm thirsty," Lisa said.

"I'm hungry," Matt said.

"All right! I get the message!" Mrs. Roberts said. "Ted, when you stop for gas, get us a cold drink."

ART of ATLANTA

Cars, Trains, and Planes

Mr. Roberts stopped for gas and bought everyone a soft drink. He drove the car a few blocks farther. Then he stopped. They were caught in a traffic jam.

"I feel as though we're going to sit here forever," Mrs. Roberts said. "And guess what I read in this book. About 150 years ago, this place was a great forest."

"Are you sure you read that?" Mr. Roberts asked.

"I read that in this little book," Mrs. Roberts said. "It's one of the best guide books I've ever read."

"Well, as long as we have to sit here, let me ask some questions," Mr. Roberts said. "Matt, Lisa, we're in the South now. How is it different from Elmville?"

"It's much hotter here," Lisa said.

Atlanta's many highways help to make it a transportation center.

"There are lots of cars like in New York," Matt said.

"And lots of planes," added Matt.

Mr. Roberts laughed. He told them they were right. Atlanta was always hot in the summer. And there were certainly lots of cars. And planes. And trains as well.

"Our little book says that Atlanta is a southeastern *crossroads* (**krôs** rōdz)," Mrs. Roberts said. "In other words, Atlanta is the *transportation* (trans pôr **tā** shən) *center* of the Southeast. Three main highways meet here. Six railroads carry goods and people in and out. And Atlanta's airport is the second busiest in our country. Planes land here from all over the world. They also fly from here to faraway cities."

Planes at Atlanta's airport carry people to places near and far.

Trains full of many goods help make
Atlanta a shipping center.

"Many southern states use Atlanta as a shipping center," Mr. Roberts said. "Farm and factory goods are sent here from all over the South. Then, they are sent out all over the world. Other goods from all parts of the earth come into Atlanta. From here, they go to the many communities of the South. Shipping goods back and forth is the job of a transportation center."

People and More People

"What else have you noticed about Atlanta?" Mr. Roberts asked.

"Well," Mrs. Roberts said, "it seems to me that there are many more people here than before. I've been here twice. Once I came when I was a little girl. Atlanta was a medium-sized city then. And I came

Many people have come to Atlanta to work in airplane *factories.*

again, ten years ago, on a visit. Even then, I could see Atlanta was growing."

"It really is growing," Mr. Roberts said. "In 25 years, the number of people has tripled. That means there are now three times as many people here. Atlanta and its suburbs now have close to 2 million people."

"Why are so many people coming here?" Lisa asked.

Mr. Roberts told her that Atlanta has many jobs to offer. And more jobs mean more people. People can work for the airlines. They can work for the railroads. They can make cars or build planes.

Until just a few years ago, most of the country around Atlanta was farmland. Then people started to think that Atlanta was a good place to do business.

They started to build their *factories* (**fak** tə rēz) in the South. A factory is a building where things are made. It wasn't long before workers moved south. They wanted to find jobs in the factories.

Mrs. Roberts said, "I also think some people are coming because the weather is mild and sunny. There are only two or three cold months. And warm, sunny days make heating bills lower."

Slowly the cars began to move. The traffic jam broke up.

"Well," Mr. Roberts said, "we have learned some things today. Atlanta is not only the capital of Georgia. It is important in other ways."

Do You Know?

1. What is a crossroads?
2. What happens in a transportation center?
3. How has Atlanta changed?
4. Why do people come to Atlanta?

Great-Aunt Kate

Mr. Roberts parked the car near a big, white house. It had a screened porch all around it. There were two magnolia (mag **nōl** yə) trees in the front yard. Pink and white flowers lined the walk. Shady trees made the place look cool.

"You'll like your Great-Aunt Kate," said Mr. Roberts. "She was a history teacher once. Now she writes books and travels."

The front door opened. A tall woman in a green dress smiled at them. Her white hair was piled high on her head. She wore pretty gold rim glasses.

"My, am I glad to see all of you!" she said, "Come on in."

They followed her inside. It was cool in the living room.

"How would you like some lemonade and iced tea?" Great-Aunt Kate asked. "I'm sure you're thirsty after such a long trip. Later, we'll have a picnic supper on the porch."

Great-Aunt Kate went for the drinks. Matt turned to his father.

"I can't understand everything Great-Aunt Kate says," he said. "Why does she sound different from us?"

Mr. Roberts laughed. "The people here speak with a southern accent. It takes a while to get used to it. We speak with a New England accent. It takes Southerners a little while to understand us also."

The Cousins Visit

Before dinner, everyone met on the porch. The Roberts saw a table filled with food. Fried chicken, potato salad, corn on the cob, and garden tomatoes were spread out. Great-Aunt Kate came from the kitchen with hot biscuits.

"Oh, this looks so good!" Mrs. Roberts said.

"Great-Aunt Kate is a great cook," Mr. Roberts said. "And her biscuits are out of this world."

"Would you like seconds?" Great-Aunt Kate asked. "We'll wait and have dessert when the kinfolk come."

"Oh? Someone is coming?" Mr. Roberts asked.

"Just a few of your cousins," said Great-Aunt Kate. "They haven't seen you in years."

"Oh, how wonderful!" said Mr. Roberts.

Half an hour later, the porch was filled with people. Everybody was smiling and remembering the old days. Matt and Lisa heard all kinds of stories about their father when he was a boy.

Great-Aunt Kate brought out peach ice cream on a tray. She told the children that Georgia is known as the Peach State. Other states raise peaches, too, she said. But Georgia has the sweetest and the biggest. The main street of Atlanta is named Peachtree Street.

After the guests left, Great-Aunt Kate sent the children to bed. Then the three grown-ups sat down and talked.

"We never forget that Ted is from the South," she said. "Family means a lot to Southerners. But I don't have to tell you about the Old South. Tomorrow, I'm going to show you the New South. Here in Atlanta, we're changing. And changing fast."

People in Atlanta are proud of their big, busy city.

Seeing Atlanta

The next morning, Great-Aunt Kate made breakfast early.

"I've finished," Lisa said. "I ate everything on my plate. What delicious bacon and eggs, Great-Aunt Kate."

"Why, thank you, Lisa," Great-Aunt Kate said. She went into the kitchen.

"I can't finish my breakfast," Matt whispered. "I can't eat the white stuff. It looks like cream of wheat. But it isn't."

Mr. Roberts looked at Matt's plate. Then he laughed.

"I should have told you about grits," he said.

This underground shopping center
and piece of art are in Atlanta.

"They are made from corn. They often come with breakfast down here. They are very good with butter."

Mr. Roberts told them that different people in different parts of the country have different foods. He was sure that Great-Aunt Kate would not like pie for breakfast. Yet many New England families serve pie in the morning.

After breakfast, Great-Aunt Kate showed the family Atlanta. They saw factories that make cars. They saw factories that make planes. They saw the office of the world's largest soft-drink business.

In downtown Atlanta, they saw a shopping center. It is called Peachtree Plaza. The hotel there has elevators on the outside of the building. Matt and Lisa

The Atlanta Braves play home baseball games in this stadium.

rode to the top and looked out on the city. From a distance, they could see how many roads meet in Atlanta.

Great-Aunt Kate pointed out that Atlanta is a center for schools. She showed them many universities. They also saw a famous medical center. Great-Aunt Kate said that the medical center is a sort of detective agency. Scientists at the center try to find out why people become sick.

At the end of the tour, Great-Aunt Kate pulled the car up to a small church on Auburn Avenue.

"When we come here, we remember Dr. Martin Luther King, Jr.," she said.

Do You Know?

1. What is Georgia's special fruit?
2. What is the name of Atlanta's main street?
3. What did Great-Aunt Kate mean when she said, "We never forget that Ted is from the South"?

Things To Do

1. Make a list of the ways you have traveled. Which ones did you like the best?
2. Tell your class a story about a visit to a relative.
3. Label on your map the Robertses' route from Washington to Atlanta.

Martin Luther King, Jr.

Great-Aunt Kate explained that Martin Luther King, Jr., was a famous American. He was born in Atlanta. As a boy, he saw black and white children going to different schools. He saw black and white people drinking from different water fountains. He saw that blacks could not sit in the front of city buses. They had to sit in the back of the bus.

When he grew up, Dr. King became a minister. He helped change things for black people.

Dr. King told his people the best way was to change things peacefully. So, he told them to stop riding the buses. For more than a year, the black

Dr. King receives the Nobel Peace Prize as Mrs. King watches.

people refused to use buses. The bus company lost money. Finally, the law was changed. Blacks could sit where they wanted.

As time went by, Dr. King helped his people solve many more problems. He taught blacks and whites to work for whatever was fair. Finally, he was given a great prize for his work. That prize is called the Nobel (nō **bel**) Peace Prize.

"Great-Aunt Kate," said Mrs. Roberts. "Do you remember something wonderful? Martin Luther King, Jr., gave a famous talk at the Lincoln Memorial in Washington."

"Who could forget it!" said Great-Aunt Kate. "He stood on the steps and said 'I have a dream.' He said those words over and over. His dream was that all people could live together and love each other. We're proud that someone from Atlanta shared that dream with his country."

Lisa listened. She remembered the Lincoln Memorial. She thought she would have liked to be there that day.

Lisa looked around the neighborhood.

"There are many black people in the South," she said. "Why are they living here? In Vermont, there are only a few."

Mrs. Roberts told her that long ago *slave* ships came to the South. A slave is a person who is owned by another person. For many years, most black people

Long ago, most Southerners lived on farms. Some were *plantations.*

in this country were slaves. They were captured and brought here from Africa. They had to work on *plantations* (plan **tā** shənz), or large farms, in the South. Later, when the slaves were freed after the Civil War, some went north. But many stayed in the South with family and friends.

"I wouldn't want to be a slave," Matt said.

"Neither would I," Lisa said.

"No one should be a slave," Mr. Roberts said. "We finally had enough sense to change all that. But it took a war and President Lincoln to make us see it was wrong. Someday, the two of you will study the Civil War. Much of the fighting took place in the South. Some of it took place right here in Atlanta."

Chicago: Transportation Center

In what ways is Chicago like Atlanta?

Can you tell why we call Chicago a transportation center?

In what ways is Chicago different from Elmville?

How are your community and Chicago alike? How are they different? Compare the transportation, buildings, and people in your community with those in Chicago.

STATE LAKE
CHICAGO

CNA
NP

Jake's Place

Before they knew it, it was time to leave Atlanta. The Robertses thanked Great-Aunt Kate for two days filled with fun and food.

Getting into the car, Mrs. Roberts said, "We're on our way. Here we come, Louisiana (loo wē zē **an** ə)."

After lunch, everyone was quiet. Suddenly Mrs. Roberts said, "Stop the car! I want some of those Georgia peaches."

"Lee! I thought the car was on fire!" Mr. Roberts said. "And all you want is peaches!"

"Your Aunt Kate told me we would be going through peach country. Please stop and buy a basket, Ted," Mrs. Roberts said.

Besides peaches, Georgia produces corn, cotton, and peanuts.

"I will as soon as we see another stand," Mr. Roberts said.

"There's one," Matt said.

"It's called Jake's Place," Mr. Roberts said. "The farm looks pretty big. There must be 20 pickers."

Mr. Roberts parked next to the *orchard* (**ôr** chərd). An orchard is land on which fruit trees grow. A man waved to them, and came over to the car. He asked how many peaches they wanted.

"Only one basket," Mr. Roberts said. "We plan to eat them along the way. We think your Georgia peaches are the best. They are so sweet and juicy."

"Why, thank you," the man said. "I like to hear that."

After being checked, these peaches will be shipped to many states.

He told them that his name was Jake Harris. He also said that his great-grandfather had been a slave. He had worked on the same land. It had been part of a big plantation then.

Later, Mr. Harris's grandfather had worked on the land. But he was not a slave. He paid money to the owner for using the land. Now Mr. Harris had bought that same bit of land. And he was making money. His peaches were the best around.

"I have an idea," Mr. Harris said. "Have your children ever picked peaches?"

"No, they haven't," Mr. Roberts said. "Matt, Lisa, do you want to try?"

Mr. Harris gave them a basket. He took them to a tree. He showed them how to pick the ripe peaches.

"If you are too rough with them, they turn brown," Mr. Harris said.

Peaches must be handled gently as they are sorted and packed.

Matt and Lisa soon had their basket full.

"Can we buy this one?" Matt asked.

"Certainly," Mr. Harris said. "And here are a few more peaches as a gift."

"Why, thank you, Mr. Harris," Mrs. Roberts said.

"Yes, thank you, Mr. Harris," Mr. Roberts said. "Maybe we'll be coming this way again. Maybe by then you'll own two orchards."

Do You Know?

1. Where was Martin Luther King, Jr., born?
2. What was one thing Dr. King helped the black people do?
3. Name a crop grown in an orchard.

To Help You Learn

Using New Words

transportation center	plantations	orchard
crossroads	factories	slaves

Read each sentence below and put in the missing word. Do not write in this book.

1. Land on which fruit trees grow is called an _____.
2. Atlanta is a transportation center and a _____.
3. _____ are places where things are made.
4. Large farms in the South were called _____.
5. _____ are persons owned by another person.
6. A _____ is where highways, railroads, and airports meet.

Talking It Over

1. Think of the communities you have visited with the Roberts family. Which one was most like Atlanta? How was it like Atlanta?
2. How will the peaches from the peach orchard reach communities all over our country?
3. What are kinfolk? Do you live in a community where kinfolk are close?
4. What was Martin Luther King, Jr.'s dream? Why is it important for all of us?

2

Gateway to the Sea

"Before we get to New Orleans," Mrs. Roberts said, "We're going to have a French lesson."

"A what?" asked Matt.

"A French lesson," Mrs. Roberts said again. "Many people in Louisiana speak French. Their *ancestors* (**an** ses tərz) came from France long ago. Ancestors are people of your family who lived before you. Now, I'm going to teach you three important words in French. They are 'yes,' 'no,' and 'thank you.' "

This outdoor restaurant in New Orleans serves French food.

"That's a good idea," Mr. Roberts said. "Everyone should know a second language. I studied French a long time ago. I wonder how much I'll remember."

"You'll find out when we get to New Orleans," Mrs. Roberts said. "We'll eat most of our meals in restaurants (**res** tə rəntz). Many of the restaurants have menus (**men** ūz) in French. A restaurant is a place to buy and eat a meal. A menu is a food list. 'Menu' and 'restaurant' are both French words."

"The word for 'yes' is 'oui' (**wē**)," Mrs. Roberts continued. "The word for 'no' is 'non' (**nō**). 'Thank you' is 'merci' (mer **sē**). Let's go over them."

Matt and Lisa said the words several times. They found they liked learning another language.

"I'll teach you more tomorrow," Mrs. Roberts promised. "Now, we have all sorts of things to learn. Let me read you something from my guide book."

Facts About New Orleans

" 'New Orleans is in the state of Louisiana near the Gulf of Mexico. A *gulf* (**gulf**) is ocean partly enclosed by land. A big river flows into the Gulf. This river is named the Mississippi (mis ə **sip** ē).

" 'New Orleans is the oldest big city in the South. About 300 years ago, a French explorer sailed down

This man catches crayfish in southern Louisiana.

the Mississippi River. He called this part of the country 'Louisiana.' He said it belonged to France. A few years later, New Orleans was built. It became the French capital of Louisiana.' "

"Don't think that Louisiana was the same size then as it is today," said Mr. Roberts. "It was a huge piece of land. It included the whole middle part of our country."

"That's right," said Mrs. Roberts. "It was so big none of the people who settled in it had ever seen it all. Settlers lived in only a tiny part of it."

Mrs. Roberts started to read her book again.

Spanish grillwork and French street signs suggest Old New Orleans.

" 'At first, French settlers came to New Orleans. Then the King of France gave Louisiana to his cousin. His cousin was the King of Spain. After that, Spanish settlers came also. The early French and Spanish settlers often married each other. Their children and grandchildren became known as Creoles (**krē** ōlz).' "

"Are there many Creoles in New Orleans now?" asked Lisa.

"Not many," said Mrs. Roberts. "But you will be able to tell that Creoles were important in New Orleans history."

"How?" asked Matt.

"Just keep your eyes and ears open," said Mrs. Roberts. "You'll hear French words being spoken. You'll read French signs. You'll see many old buildings that look Spanish."

"Better keep your mouth open too," said Mr. Roberts. "New Orleans is famous for its Creole cooking. Many restaurants serve Creole foods. They are a spicy mixture of French and Spanish dishes."

"Oh, Ted," Mrs. Roberts said. "You're making me hungry. But we have one more important thing to read about before we stop."

The Louisiana Purchase

Mrs. Roberts told the children that France took Louisiana back from Spain after about 40 years. Soon afterwards, the United States bought the land from France. This sale became known as the Louisiana Purchase. A purchase is something bought. Fifteen of our states were made out of the Louisiana Purchase. It was the largest piece of land our country ever got.

Do You Know?

1. Other than English, what language do many people in Louisiana speak?
2. Who are Creoles?
3. What was the largest piece of land our country ever got?

Pirate Country

Mr. Roberts pulled the car up to a small cabin. Everyone got out.

"This isn't New Orleans," said Matt.

"No," said Mr. Roberts. "Mom and I have a surprise for you. We've rented a cabin in pirate country. This is it."

"Oh, Dad! That's great," Matt said. "But what about pirates? Are they still here?"

Mr. Roberts smiled. "Not any more," he said. "But there were lots of them here over 150 years ago. One of their leaders was Jean Lafitte (**jon** la **fēt**). Lafitte ran a blacksmith shop in New Orleans. He used to meet his pirate crew on a small island. The island is

Jean Lafitte, shown here, once owned this blacksmith shop.

in the Mississippi River near the city. They would make their plans on the island. Then they would sail into the Gulf of Mexico and attack ships. They took the goods the ships carried."

"He sounds like a scary person," said Lisa.

"Yes," said her father, "in a way he was. But he also became a sort of hero. At one time, ships from Great Britain carried soldiers to New Orleans. These soldiers were going to attack New Orleans. They were fighting the Americans. The British tried to pay Jean Lafitte to help them. Instead, Lafitte went to help the Americans. They were led by General Andrew Jackson. With help from Lafitte and his pirates, General Jackson won."

In the Battle of New Orleans, Lafitte helped the Americans.

"Did Jean Lafitte stop being a pirate, then?" Matt asked.

"No," laughed his father. "He went right back to his old tricks."

The Robertses' cabin was on a country road. Down the road was a wide, muddy river. "Tomorrow," said Mrs. Roberts, "we'll go and have a look at the mighty Mississippi."

The Mighty Mississippi

The next morning, the Roberts family got up early. After breakfast, they drove to the river. Mr. Roberts parked the car.

"Why are we stopping here?" Lisa asked.

The Mississippi River is one of the world's great trade waterways.

"Lisa, Matt. I want to show you something," he said. "Here is a good view of the Mississippi River. Mississippi is an Indian word. It means 'great river.'

"The Mississippi River flows into the Gulf of Mexico from the north. It starts near Canada. Two hundred and fifty other rivers flow into it. The Mississippi and the rivers that flow into it make up the Mississippi River System. This great river system touches 31 of our 50 states.

"The land through which the river flows is called the Mississippi River Valley. The river collects rich soil as it flows through the valley. It drops this soil south of

A picture of the Mississippi River from the air shows how it winds.

New Orleans. The soil is making Louisiana bigger and bigger."

"Dad," Lisa said, "doesn't the Mississippi River ever flood?"

"Sometimes it does," said her father. "Let's see what engineers have done to control the flooding."

They got into the car again. This time they drove several miles away from the river. Mr. Roberts stopped the car on a hill. Lisa and Matt could see the river far away across flat grassland. The long hill they were on followed the direction of the river. It went as far as they could see both ways.

Mr. Roberts told them they were standing on a *levee* (**lev** ē). Levees are made from earth. Some are as high as three-story or four-story buildings. They are made to control floods. Sometimes, the levees are built far away from the river. Then the river can spread out when it fills with water. It covers the low land next to the river. This land is called the *flood plain*. But the levees keep the river from flooding towns and cities.

"Are levees able to stop all the flooding, Ted?" asked Mrs. Roberts.

"No," said Mr. Roberts. "Even after levees were built, floods were a problem for New Orleans.

"Part of the city is lower than the level of the sea. The river level is higher than part of New Orleans.

"But the flood problem was finally solved. A *spillway* was built. It connects the river to a large lake

Some levees are strengthened with concrete.

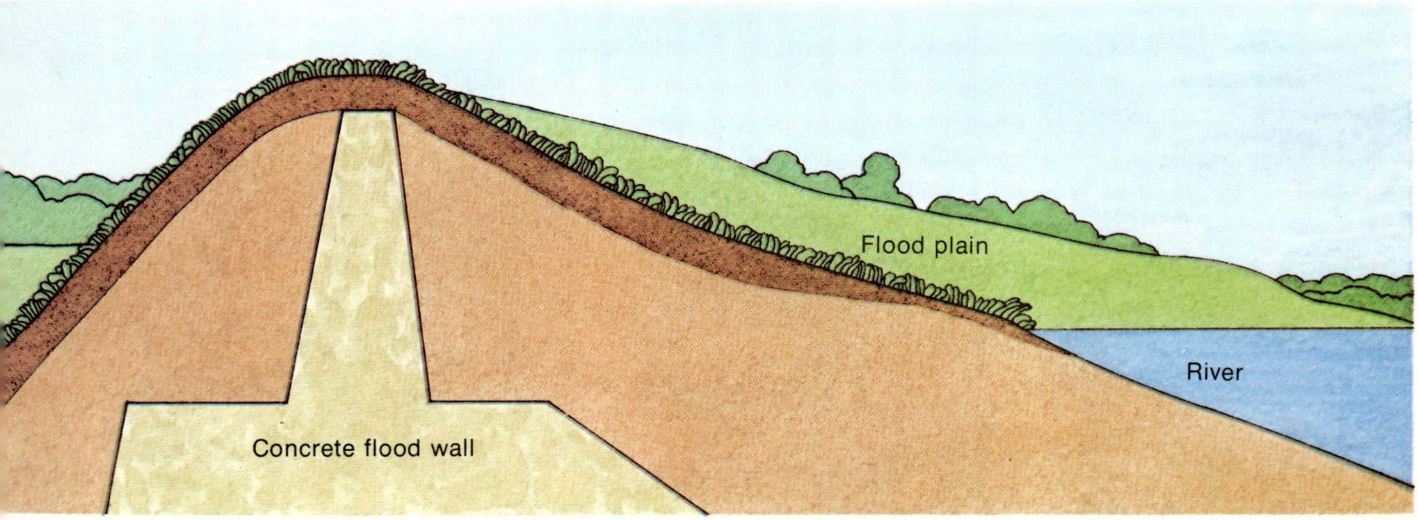

near the city. When the river floods, the extra water goes through the spillway. The spillway carries the water to the lake. Let's drive on to New Orleans and see it."

The Roberts family drove to Lake Pontchartrain (**pän** chər trān) in New Orleans.

"This is where the spillway dumps the flood water," said Mr. Roberts.

"Wow!" said Lisa. "This is a big lake. And this bridge is the longest I've ever seen. We've been driving on it over half an hour."

"This is the longest bridge in the world," said Mr. Roberts. "It connects New Orleans with its northern suburbs."

"What a wonderful sight!" said Mr. Roberts. "Now, let's go see another exciting sight, the docks."

Do You Know?

1. What is a levee?
2. Why does New Orleans need a spillway?
3. What is the Mississippi River System?

Things To Do

1. Color in the Mississippi River on your outline map.
2. Make a drawing to show how the Mississippi River is connected to Lake Pontchartrain.

LYKES LINES

An Inland Port

The Robertses parked their car. Then they walked to the docks. On the docks, they watched people carrying big boxes. They watched machines lifting huge bundles onto ships.

New Orleans is one of the world's busiest ports. In our country, only the port of New York City is busier. But the port of New Orleans is different from the port of New York. New Orleans is an inland port. It is on the river, and not on the ocean. Ships must go about 100 miles (160 kilometers) down the river to reach the Gulf of Mexico.

An inland port makes loading and unloading ships easy. On the ocean, strong winds may make the water rough. Then it is hard to bring the ships near the land. But the waters of an inland port are usually smooth.

Ships from all over the world come to New Orleans. Many of these ships come from South America. They bring such goods as bananas, cocoa beans, and coffee. Ships take away such goods as grain and other foods.

New Orleans is also a busy port for barges. Barges are boats without motors that carry goods. They are often joined together. Another boat with a strong engine moves them along. Barges go up and down the Mississippi River. Some bring grain and other food south from the Midwest. Others carry oil and other goods north from New Orleans.

New Orleans is one of the world's busiest inland *ports*.

Barges also travel between New Orleans and the Gulf Coast. A *coast* (**kōst**) is land on the edge of water. Many barges carry oil from the coast to the city. Both the coastland and the ocean floor have many oil wells.

"Well," said Mrs. Roberts at the day's end, "I've seen the Mississippi. I've seen the docks. Next, I want to see New Orleans itself."

The French Quarter

The next day, the family took a tour. They decided to go by surrey. A surrey is a fancy wagon pulled by a horse. The surrey took them to the French Quarter. It is the old part of the city. There, they joined a group of tourists. A tourist is someone who takes a trip for fun.

Many people tour the French Quarter in a surrey.

A guide showed the tourists some buildings over 200 years old. Many had beautiful balconies. The balconies often had iron grillwork on them. It looked like lace. They saw tiny gardens behind the houses. They walked down narrow streets with French names.

The guide pointed out a beautiful old church. It faces Jackson Square. The square was named for Andrew Jackson. He became a hero after he won the Battle of New Orleans. Later, he became President of the United States. The guide also pointed out Jean Lafitte's blacksmith shop.

The Roberts also saw the building where the Louisiana Purchase took place. Then they went through the Mardi Gras (**märd ē grä**) Museum. They saw lots of colorful costumes.

St. Louis Cathedral is a beautiful old church in the French Quarter.

The King of Mardi Gras rides in a parade on a colorful float.

"Oh," said Mrs. Roberts. "Just think what the French Quarter must be like during Mardi Gras!"

"What's Mardi Gras?" asked Matt.

"Mardi Gras," said Mrs. Roberts, "is the end of a winter celebration. The celebration lasts four to eight weeks. All that time, there are parties and dances. On the last day, a king is chosen. He leads a wonderful parade. All the people in the parade and on the floats wear costumes. They toss toys and gold-colored coins to the crowds."

"That sounds great," said Matt. "I'd like to see Mardi Gras."

After the tour, the Robertses returned to their motel. On the way, they saw more of the city. They drove along St. Charles Street and Canal Street. They

People in New Orleans use street cars instead of *subway* trains.

saw railroad tracks in the street. Then they saw a streetcar running along the tracks.

Not far from Canal Street, they saw the Superdome. This building is almost as long as two football fields. It can seat 100,000 people at a time. Football, baseball, and basketball games are played there.

Near the river, they saw a large *convention* (kən **ven** shən) hall. A convention is a meeting. Many groups of people hold their meetings in New Orleans. They get together to solve problems. After their meetings they enjoy being tourists in the city.

After the tour, Mrs. Roberts said, "One thing is clear. New Orleans is a beautiful and important city. It is a center for both trade and tourism."

San Francisco: Many People Living by the Bay

New Orleans and San Francisco are both busy port cities.

New Orleans and San Francisco have famous streets and buildings. But their people are even more important. Why?

Find some of these people in the pictures of San Francisco.

They are Americans. Americans are one people from many lands.

Creative
ORIGAMI
XEROX

Where Jazz Began

That evening after dinner, the family walked around the French Quarter. The night was warm, but not hot.

"Our Creole dinner was delicious," said Mrs. Roberts. "I especially liked the shrimp and rice dish. Only one thing could make me happier. Follow me."

She led Matt, Lisa, and Mr. Roberts through the narrow streets. They went through a gate of iron bars. They entered a room filled with long wooden benches. On the benches sat men and women. They were laughing and smiling and clapping. The Robertses found some empty places and sat down.

"There's a band," whispered Matt.

In front of the room were five men. Four were black and one was white. Each man had an instrument (**in** strə mənt). At the piano sat a woman.

"She has bells on her legs," whispered Lisa.

The band began to play. When the woman moved her legs, the bells jingled. Some of the songs were fast. Some were slow. The people swayed to the music. Sometimes they stamped their feet. Sometimes they clapped along with the music.

When it was time to go, Lisa looked once more at the band.

"That music was sad and happy all at the same time," she said. "It was wonderful!"

These musicians were a famous
New Orleans jazz band long ago.

"It was jazz, honey," explained Mr. Roberts. "Jazz began here in New Orleans. Now it's played all over the world. But I think it still sounds best here."

Do You Know?

1. What is an inland port?
2. Where do the barges in the port of New Orleans go?
3. What is Mardi Gras? When is it?
4. What kind of music is New Orleans famous for?

To Help You Learn

Using New Words

gulf — levee — spillway
flood plain — ancestors — coast
convention

Match each word above with one of the meanings below. Be sure you find the right meaning for each word.

1. People in your family who lived before you
2. Ocean partly enclosed by land
3. A hill made of earth, built to control floods
4. Something built to let extra water flow away without causing flooding
5. Land at the edge of water
6. A meeting
7. Low land next to a river which sometimes floods

Talking It Over

1. How is New Orleans different from Atlanta? How is it like Atlanta?
2. How does the Mississippi River help people who live along its banks? What harm can it do?
3. Why is New Orleans called a "Gateway to the Sea"? How is its port like and unlike New York's?
4. The ancestors of some people living in New Orleans came from France. Where did your ancestors come from? Can you find these places on a globe?

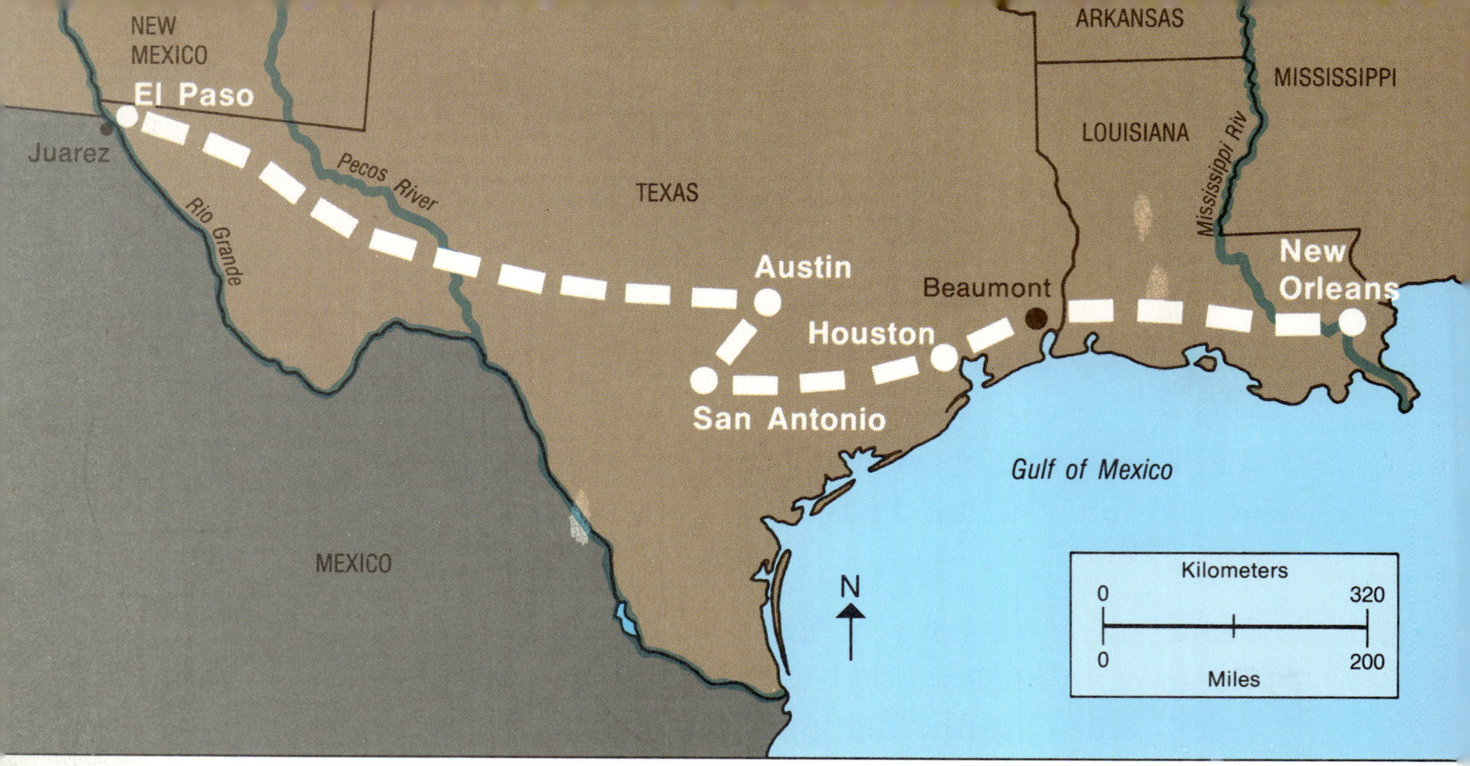

3

Border Communities

The Robertses left New Orleans and drove west along the Gulf of Mexico. Soon they had crossed the *border* (**bôr** dər) into Texas. A border is where one place stops and another begins. On a map, it is shown as a line. Mrs. Roberts turned to ask the children a question.

"What comes to mind when you hear the word Texas?" she said.

"Cowboys," said Matt.

"Wide open spaces," said Lisa.

"Yes, I suppose everybody thinks cowboys and open spaces belong in Texas," Mrs. Roberts said. "But how about big business? How about big, modern cities?"

"Does Texas have those things, too?" asked Matt.

"It certainly does," said Mr. Roberts. "And you'll soon see one reason why."

Oil Country

The car neared the city of Beaumont (**bō** mont). Suddenly, the children saw a strange sight. Scattered over the fields were large pumps. They rocked back and forth with a steady beat.

These pumps bring up oil after the natural flow has stopped.

"See those!" said Mr. Roberts. "They help make Texas rich."

"What are they?" Lisa asked.

"They are pumps," said Mr. Roberts. "They lift *crude oil* (**krōōd oil**) from the ground."

Mr. Roberts said that the land near Beaumont was full of crude oil. In fact, he said, the first oil well in Texas, Spindletop, was drilled near Beaumont. It started to gush, or flow, over 75 years ago. Such an oil well is sometimes called a "gusher." Since then, hundreds of oil wells have been drilled in Texas.

When people drill for oil, they build a *derrick* (**der** ik). The oil stops flowing by itself. Then, a big

This diagram shows the important parts of an oil pump.

pump is used to bring the oil up. This crude oil is taken to a factory called a *refinery* (ri **fīn** ər ē). At the refinery, the crude oil is made into *fuel* (**fyū** əl) oil. Fuel runs machines and heats buildings.

Texas also gives our country *natural* (**nach** ə rəl) *gas*. Natural gas is also a fuel. It is often found in the same well that has crude oil.

As they drove, the family saw more oil wells. They even saw derricks in the Gulf waters near Houston (**hū** stən). Oil has helped make Houston the

This *derrick* is over an oil well in the Gulf of Mexico.

largest city in Texas. It is an important center for oil and gas refining.

"Texas must have enough oil to last forever," said Lisa.

"Not true," said Mr. Roberts. "Our leaders tell us that we do not have enough oil. Even now, we buy it from other countries. We must save as much as possible. We must find new ways to heat our homes. New ways to run our machines."

"How can we do that?" asked Matt.

"There are many ways," his mother said. "We can drive smaller cars. We can drive them more slowly. We can turn off TVs and air conditioners when not using them. We can keep our houses cooler in winter. We can even learn to use the sun's rays to heat buildings."

"I don't think anybody in Texas will have to use the sun for heating," said Lisa. "It's very warm here. I can't believe it gets very cold."

"Certain parts of the state do get cold," said her mother. "But maybe the warmer parts can use the sun's energy to cool their buildings instead."

Do You Know?

1. How is crude oil taken out of the ground?
2. Where is crude oil turned into fuel?
3. What is natural gas?
4. What are some ways people can save oil and gas?

Stephen F. Austin

Lisa's Log

Austin, Texas

Thursday, August 25

Matt got sick in San Antonio. He feels better now. Today we drove to Austin. Austin is the capital of Texas. We saw the University of Texas. We saw the capitol building. That part of the city is beautiful. It was planned, just like Washington, D.C.

A student told us that Austin was named after a famous pioneer. He was Stephen F. Austin. He came to Texas over 150 years ago. He brought along 300 other families. At that time, Texas was not a state. It belonged to Mexico.

Mr. Austin's settlers were the first people here from the United States. They led the way for all the others.

Oh yes, one more thing. Mr. Austin's family came from New England. He went to school in Connecticut. You <u>could</u> say he came from New England to Texas. Just like us!

Tales about the American cowboy
are famous all over the world.

Pecos Bill

Lisa and Matt were hot and tired. It seemed as if they had been driving forever. The road looked like a thin ribbon. It stretched over the wide, flat land. Here and there were dry ditches. Low bushes and trees dotted the plains. When the Robertses crossed the Pecos (**pā** cōs) River, the scenery changed. They began to see gray, stony mountains. Mrs. Roberts turned to the children.

"Seeing the Pecos River reminds me of a *tall tale.* Texas is famous for this sort of make-believe story. Have you ever heard of Pecos Bill?" she asked.

"Was he a cowboy?" asked Lisa.

"More than a cowboy," Mrs. Roberts said. "He was a kind of supercowboy!" Mrs. Roberts picked up a book and began to read. Matt and Lisa listened carefully.

" 'Pecos Bill was quite a man. He was born in East Texas. His family traveled west in a wagon. There were many children. On the trip, Pecos Bill fell out of the wagon. He was raised by an animal called a coyote (**kī** ōt). He was taught most things by a bear. Later, he became a cowboy. He taught everyone how to rope cows and ride ponies. One day, he roped a mountain lion. He whipped it with a rattlesnake. He rode it into a camp of bad men. They were so scared that they made him the boss.

" 'During a dry spell, Pecos Bill dug a river called the Rio Grande (**rē** ō **grand**).' "

"Hey," said Mr. Roberts, "we'll be seeing the Rio Grande before long."

"I wish I could have seen Pecos Bill dig the river," said Matt.

"Matt, dear," said Mrs. Roberts "Pecos Bill didn't really make the Rio Grande. Rainfall makes rivers. Remember, I told you this story was a tall tale."

Cowboys of the Past

Mr. Roberts told the children how many tall tales in Texas started. They were made up, he said, by lonely cowboys. A long time ago, cowboys worked with

A cowboy on the *range* needs to know a lot about horses and cattle.

longhorns. Longhorns are cattle. They were first brought here by the Spanish. The cowboys used to say that they were "tough to eat and tougher to handle."

The longhorns roamed over open, or unfenced, *ranges* (**rānj** əz). A range is a large field where cattle feed on grass. Once a year, cowboys rounded up the cattle. Then they drove them to shipping points in the North. This trip was called a *cattle drive*. In Kansas (**kan** zəs) or Missouri (mə **zŭr** ē), the cattle were put on railroad cars. Trains carried them to meat-packing cities like Chicago.

At one time, a Wild West Show was as popular as the circus is today.

Roundups and cattle drives were lonely for cowboys. As they sat around campfires, they told stories to pass the time. And they sang songs to keep the cattle quiet.

"Do cowboys still make cattle drives?" asked Matt.

"Not often, any more," said Mr. Roberts. "Now, there are railroads and highways all over Texas. Raising cattle has changed a lot since the old days."

Mr. Roberts thought for a minute. Then he said, "Matt, Lisa, would you like to see a *ranch*? A ranch is a large farm with grazing land where cattle, sheep, and horses are raised. I have an old friend who has a ranch near the Pecos River. He has invited us to visit."

Do You Know?

1. Who was Stephen F. Austin?
2. What is a roundup?
3. What is a ranch?
4. Who first brought longhorns into the country?

Things To Do

1. Find a tall tale to tell to your classmates. Make it up, if you like.
2. What was Pecos Bill like? What words would you use to describe him?

Cowboys of Today

"This is quite a ranch," Mr. Roberts said. "We have been driving on your land for half an hour."

He was talking to Clint Baker. Mr. Baker owned the Lazy R Ranch. He also owned cattle and horses.

Mr. Baker talked about the cattle business. He explained that longhorns aren't raised anymore. Other kinds of cattle have more tender meat. Cattle don't roam the open range anymore, either. They are kept behind fences. They don't feed on grass as much as before. Now many ranchers grow special foods to feed the cattle.

Cowboys still ride horses, but not often to round up cattle. They do that in jeeps. They sometimes use helicopters (**hel** ə kop tərz) to look for lost cows.

Texas ranchers have replaced longhorns with cattle like these.

"Don't worry, kids," said Mr. Baker. "Cowboys still wear ten-gallon hats and high-heeled boots. They still know how to handle cattle and horses. And they still think of the range as their home."

Spanish Lesson

The sun was high in the sky when the Robertses left the Lazy R Ranch. They drove toward the city of El Paso (el **pas** ō).

"I think it's time for another language lesson," said Mr. Roberts. "El Paso is next door to Mexico. And many people in El Paso speak Spanish. Lee, can you remember a few words?"

"Yes, I think I can," she said. " 'Yes' is 'si' (**sē**). 'No' is just like English. It's 'no' (**nô**). And to say 'thank you' you say 'gracias' (**grä** sē äs)."

"We also know 'adios,' the word for 'goodbye,' " said Lisa. "Mr. Alvarez taught us that word in Washington."

"Now, just two more words," said Mr. Roberts. "Can anybody tell me what 'Rio Grande' means in Spanish?"

"Well," said Lisa, " 'Grande' sounds just like our word 'grand.' Is that what it means?"

"Close," said Mr. Roberts. "Actually, it means 'great.' "

"And 'Rio' means 'river,' " said Mrs. Roberts.

"So 'Rio Grande' means 'great river,' " said Lisa.

A photograph shows you only a small part of the Rio Grande.

The Rio Grande

The Roberts family decided to stop and look at the Rio Grande. Mr. Roberts said that this river is part of the border between the United States and Mexico.

Matt and Lisa looked at the river. Matt said, "It's pretty wide, but it doesn't look very deep."

"Parts of the Rio Grande are not deep enough for boats," said Mr. Roberts. "But the part near the Gulf of Mexico is deeper."

Mrs. Roberts said, "You know what the Texans say? They say the Rio Grande is so muddy it's too thin to plow and too thick to drink."

"There's some truth to that," Mr. Roberts said. "But up in New Mexico, the Rio Grande is clear and clean. The water flows in ditches to the fields."

Do You Know?

1. Why aren't longhorns raised today?
2. What does "Rio Grande" mean in English?
3. The Rio Grande is part of the border between what two countries?

Things To Do

1. Share some foreign words with your class.
2. Draw a picture to show what Texas is like.

A Spanish Mission

The Robertses stopped at Ysleta (is **let** täh). They saw a little church. Its mud walls were beige (**bāzh**) like the earth.

"This little church is called a *mission* (**mish** ən)," said Mrs. Roberts. "It was built by Indians about 300 years ago. Spanish priests showed them how to build it."

Lisa and Matt learned that the Spanish came to the Southwest over 400 years ago. Spanish soldiers rode up on horses from deep in Mexico. They had heard

The Spanish were the first Europeans to explore the Southwest.

many tales about cities of gold. They wanted to find these riches. Later, Spanish priests came to the Southwest. They wanted the Indians of the Southwest to become Christians. So they built churches. Near the churches, the soldiers built forts. Around the churches and forts, other buildings were put up. These little communities were called missions. Indians came to the missions. Many of them learned Spanish and became Christians. But they kept many old ways, too.

"In El Paso," said Mrs. Roberts, "you will hear a lot of Spanish."

A sheepherder tends his flock outside an old Spanish *mission.*

Near El Paso, farmers grow cotton and ranchers raise cattle.

El Paso's Five C's

El Paso, the Robertses were told, is growing fast. Like Atlanta, it is a transportation center. Railroads and highways meet here. Many goods go in and out. Today, El Paso has nearly 400,000 people.

The Robertses were surprised to find El Paso full of factories.

"Remember New York City?" asked Mrs. Roberts. "Here, too, factories make garments. They make jeans, slacks, and children's clothes."

"People in El Paso like to say their business is the Five C's," said Mr. Roberts. "The Five C's are clothing, cattle, climate, cotton, and copper. Much of

Traffic is busy between Juarez and El Paso.

our country's copper comes from El Paso's refineries. And cotton became an important crop after a dam was built. The irrigated land is right for growing cotton."

Matt and Lisa knew that El Paso was called a border city. "What does that mean?" asked Matt.

"Well," said Mr. Roberts, "many Hispanics, or Spanish-speaking people, work in El Paso. Some of them have always lived here. Others come over the border from Mexico. Mexico is across the border from El Paso."

Mrs. Roberts got out her guide book. "It says here," she said, "that many Mexicans coming to El Paso cross the Rio Grande from Juarez (**hwär** es).

People visit Mexico from El Paso by crossing a bridge.

Juarez is in Mexico. Three bridges join Juarez and El Paso. A streetcar runs over one of them."

"It also says," she went on, "that many Americans cross the Rio Grande from El Paso to go to Juarez. Many of these people are tourists." Mrs. Roberts smiled. "How would you like to take a trip to Juarez?"

"Oh, neat!" said Lisa. "I'd like that."

The Roberts family decided to take the streetcar.

As they crossed the bridge, they saw Mexican children going the other way. They asked the guard where the children were going.

"Those children go to school in El Paso," he said. "They go over the bridge twice a day."

A tourist in Mexico sometimes sees colorful dancers like these.

In a few hours, the Robertses rode back to the United States. Mr. and Mrs. Roberts came back with some Mexican pots. Lisa and Matt brought salted pumpkin seeds.

"That was fun," said Lisa. "And so easy. Now I can say I have visited another country."

Do You Know?

1. Why did Spanish soldiers come to the Southwest?
2. What is a mission?
3. What is the city across the border from El Paso? In which country is it?

To Help You Learn

Using New Words

derrick	mission	natural gas
range	border	crude oil
fuel	ranch	tall tale
refinery	cattle drive	

Make two columns on your paper. Title one column "Oil." Title the other column "Cattle."

Look at the words above. Some of them have to do with oil. Some of them have to do with cattle. Other words are about other things.

First, write the words about oil in the oil column. Then write the words about cattle in the cattle column.

Now, write a sentence to explain the meaning of each word that is left over.

Talking It Over

1. Why is the crude oil business important to Texans? Why is it important to the whole country?
2. What can we do to make the oil in our country last longer? Why should we try to do something?
3. What is a tall tale? Why do people think up tall tales? Can you remember one about Pecos Bill? Make up your own tall tale about him.
4. How has cattle ranching changed?
5. In what ways is the Southwest still Spanish?

To Help You Learn

Activities: Gathering Facts About Community Workers

You have seen how people work in many communities. All communities have many kinds of work.

In each community, some people are teachers. Some are doctors or workers in offices. Other people build roads and buildings. Some people drive trucks and trains. They carry goods from one place to another. Others load and unload ships. Some people make things in factories. Others sell things in stores.

Find out how different people make a living in your community. Visit the places of business on one block of your community.

Ask someone in each place what kind of work is done there.

Write down what you learn.

Count the number of people who do each kind of job.

Tell how each job is important to the whole community.

UNIT 4

New and Old Communities

You have visited many communities with the Roberts family. Most of these communities have been built where there is plenty of rainfall. In this unit, you will see a different sort of community.

Looking at the Pictures

Look at the pictures of desert communities on these two pages. In what ways do they look different from other communities in this book?

Which photograph shows a community that has changed the land? In what way was the land changed? What made the change possible?

Looking Ahead

What kinds of communities have grown in the desert?

How does the land around a community make it the way it is?

Words to Watch For

Look at the words below. As you read, you will find out what they mean. You will find out how to say them. Look in the Word List, too.

ceremony	custom	future	reservation
climate	drought	pueblo	reservoir

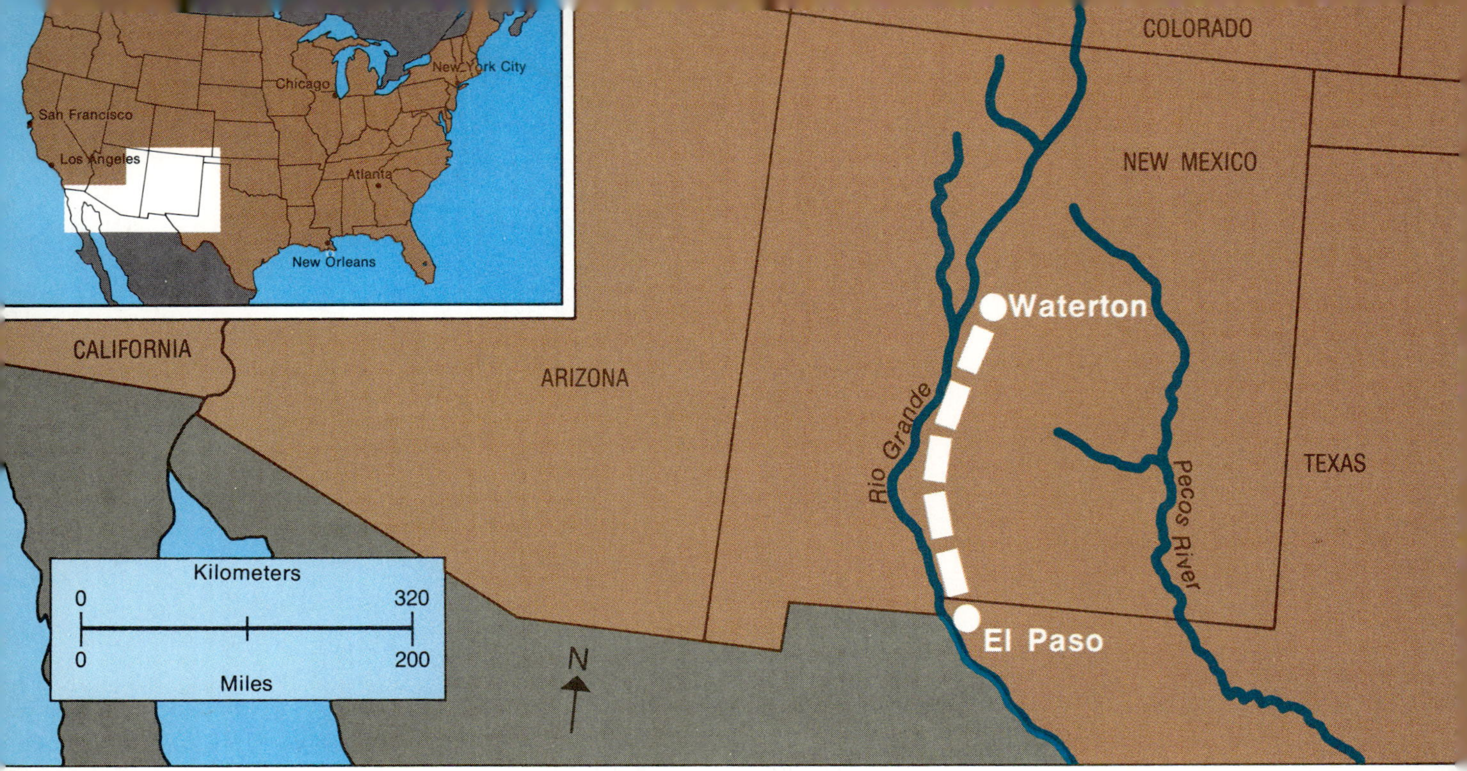

1

Planning a New Community

Matt couldn't sit still any longer. He wriggled around in the car.

"Are we here? Are we really here?" he asked.

"Yes, Matt," Mr. Roberts answered. "We're in New Mexico at last."

"Then stop the car. We can start being pioneers right now."

"Not yet, Matt," Mr. Roberts said. "New Mexico is a big state. We must go where the dam will be built."

The Roberts family drove on. They had traveled through many states. They had seen many different places. Matt remembered the small farm in New England. The farmer there grew many fruits and vegetables. There is rain in that part of the country for crops to grow. Then Matt thought about New Jersey. There, the truck farms were very large. Those farmers also have all the water they need. Lisa thought about the cranberry bogs. The ground there had been wet and spongy.

But they had seen more than farms on their trip. They had driven through the lovely Appalachian Mountains. The mountains were covered with trees.

What differences do you see between these two places?

They had traveled through deep valleys. They had crossed wide rivers. Wherever they had been, they had seen green lands and rushing waters.

Parts of New Mexico are like that, too. In the north of New Mexico are the Rocky Mountains. Thick forests of fir and pine trees grow there. Eastern New Mexico has the Great Plains (**plānz**). *Plains* are flat stretches of land. Grass grows on the plains. Large herds of sheep and cattle are raised there. The Pecos River runs through eastern New Mexico. Near the river is a beautiful valley where fruit is grown. Some places in New Mexico get enough water for plants to grow.

Mountain *streams* look different from the dry *desert.*

The Desert

It is different in the desert. A lot of New Mexico is desert. The rain comes mostly in sudden, heavy thundershowers. It comes in the afternoon in July and August. With little water, different kinds of plants grow. One of them is the cactus (**kak** tus). The cactus stores water in its stems and branches. The desert grass is not green. It is gray and silver. When it does rain, the desert is suddenly covered with flowers.

Lisa looked out the car window. In every direction she looked, she could see mountains. It was summer. But the tops of some of them were white with snow. High in the mountains it is always cold.

Desert plants and flowers grow without much water.

The car was on a bumpy road near a river. But the river didn't look like others the Robertses had seen. Not like the Mississippi River or the Potomac River. The water was very low. It looked as if the river would soon be dry.

"How can we live here?" Lisa asked. "Will we be able to get what we need?"

"Yes," Mrs. Roberts answered. "And remember, one of our basic needs is shelter. We're going to get that right now."

They came to a town. It was the town closest to where the dam would be. There were a few stores. There was also a sign that said "Mobile Homes." It was just what they were looking for. Mr. Roberts stopped the car. Matt was the first one to get out.

"Look at all these mobile homes. I like this one," Matt said. He pointed to the largest home on the lot.

"I don't think we need one that big," laughed Mr. Roberts. "Let's look at all of them before we make a decision."

A tall young man came out of the office. "I'm Billy Chee (**chē**)," he said. "May I help you?"

"We're going to live in a mobile home park," Mrs. Roberts explained. "We need a home until the dam is built."

"I'll show you what we have," Mr. Chee said. "I heard about the dam. It will be a good thing for my people."

These Indians work as welders at a *factory* outside the *reservation.*

At the Mobile Home Lot

Billy Chee explained that he was a Navajo (**näv** ə hō). Navajos are an Indian tribe. Most of his people live on a *reservation* (**rez** ər **vā** shən). A reservation is land that has been set aside for the Indians to live on. Long ago, each tribe lived where it wanted. Then the pioneers came. The Indians and the pioneers each wanted the land. Finally the Indians were forced to live on reservations.

"Will your people leave their reservation?" Lisa asked. "Will they leave to work on the dam?"

"Well," Mr. Chee answered, "many Indians do work outside their reservations. But they travel back and forth to work."

"Do you live on a reservation?" Matt asked.

This small town in New Mexico is home for some Navajos.

"I live here in town. Not all Indians live on the reservation. But I go there often. I like to visit my family."

"Could I ever go there?" Matt asked.

"You can all go," Mr. Chee said to the Roberts family. "The next time I go back, I'll take you with me."

"Thank you," Mr. Roberts said. "We'd like that. Now, let's choose our new home."

Do You Know?

1. What kind of land covers most of New Mexico?
2. What is a reservation?
3. What tribe does Billy Chee belong to?

The New Land

After they ate, Lisa and Matt had time to look around. The camp was in a low place. It was in the shade of big trees. Their roots got water from the river.

"They are called cottonwoods," said Mrs. Roberts.

The children could see why New Mexico is called the Land of Enchantment. The desert was bright with

The *desert* is a land of clear air, bright sunshine, and little water.

sunlight. The air was very dry and clear. It was possible to see a long way in every direction.

"You know," Mrs. Roberts said, "most people think all deserts are hot. The air is very clear, and the land heats quickly in the sunlight. It also cools quickly when the sun goes down. Then, the air gets cold. We'll be wearing sweaters at night. Even in the summer, nights are cool in the desert."

Matt picked up a rock. It was lying in the sunlight. He dropped it quickly. It was very hot. He picked up another rock from under a bush. It felt cool.

"I see what you mean," he said. "The shade is like the night. That's why this rock is cool."

Not many people were in the mobile home park yet. By the end of the week, everyone would arrive. Now it was a quiet place. Lisa thought of New York City. That had not been at all quiet. Subways, cars, trucks, and buses roared. Great ships sailed in and out of the busy harbor. But here, the river wasn't deep enough for a canoe.

Matt kicked the sand. "There's nothing here," he said, to no one special.

"Just wait," Lisa said. "When the dam is finished, this land will look different. Remember the Mississippi River Valley? The land there had plenty of water. Someday, this desert will have water, too."

At last, Matt felt like a pioneer. He was part of a group that was doing something important.

The Mobile Home Community

Before long, Matt saw a lot of changes. Many mobile homes filled the park. Each family was shown where to place its home. The homes were lined up in rows. There was a wide space between each row. Mr. Roberts' company had made a plan for the park. Mr. Roberts' company knew the park needed a plan. Without it, people would place their homes in every direction. With a planned space for each home, the park looked like a small town. The open spaces between the rows of homes were like streets.

The mobile home park was a planned community, like Washington, D.C., our country's capital. The community was planned by the company that was building the dam.

At this mobile home park there is a special place for each home.

The company picked the place for the park. Before they did, they made a list that helped them find a good spot. This is what they looked for.

1. The community had to be near the dam.
2. It had to be in a place where a road could be built.
3. There had to be enough flat space for all the mobile homes.
4. It had to be near water.
5. It had to be near some trees. It had to be protected from the wind.

The people from the company studied the land. At last they found the best place. Now the Roberts family and many others could live there.

Do You Know?

1. Why did Matt feel like a real pioneer?
2. Why did Mr. Roberts's company need a plan for the mobile home park?
3. Tell three things Mr. Roberts's company looked for in choosing a place for the mobile home park.

Things To Do

1. Cut out pictures of desert flowers and field flowers. Make two shows on the bulletin board.
2. Draw a picture of the mobile home park. Mark the Robertses' spot.

Many people work to build a town.
They meet to talk about their *plans.*

Planning a New Town

The park was just a beginning. It would be three or more years before the dam would be finished. Many of the people in the park would go on to different jobs. But other people would come to live there. New homes would be built. Stores would open to sell the things people need. A town would begin to grow in the middle of the desert.

Lisa wondered how a town begins. Right now, she saw nothing but earth and rocks.

But several people were thinking ahead. They were planning the town already, as L'Enfant had planned Washington. They wanted to be sure the new community would have enough space. They didn't want it be a crowded place. When a city is crowded, too many people and buildings are too close together.

Every *community* has special groups that make decisions.

The planners called a meeting. The people from the mobile home park came to the meeting.

The next day, Lisa and Matt asked what had happened. "First," Mrs. Roberts said, "the *chairperson* (**chār** pər sun) said we must study the land. We have to find the best place for the town."

"What is a chairperson?" asked Matt.

"A chairperson is a person who is in charge of a meeting," answered Mrs. Roberts. "Our chairperson asked questions to start off the meeting."

Mrs. Roberts said the chairperson then asked, "What buildings will there be? What things will the town need?"

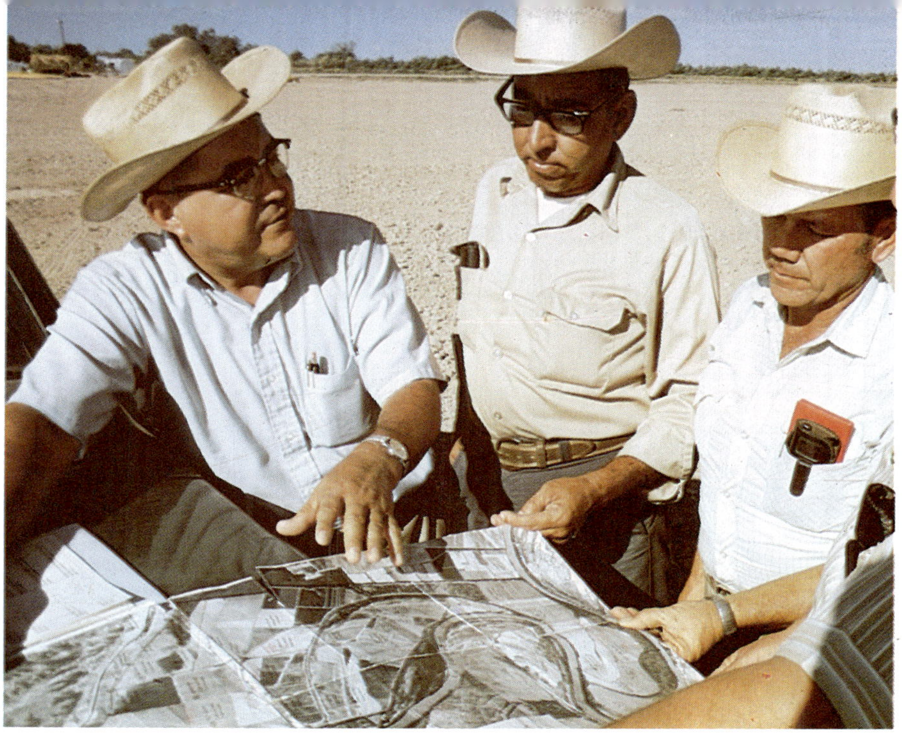

These city planners are deciding how best to use the land.

Matt thought. "I know what I think," he said. "A school, a library, and a movie theater."

"O. K., Matt, what else?" said Mrs. Roberts.

Matt thought, but he wasn't sure.

"Well," said Mrs. Roberts, "we decided we'll also need a fire department, a police station, a shopping center, a bus station, and a medical building."

"You forgot something," said Lisa. "A city needs more than buildings. I think it should have a real park. It should be a place where people can walk and sit. It should be a place where kids can play."

"Yes, Lisa," said her mother. "Someone suggested a park, too."

A *community* needs houses, fire departments, and places to vote.

The most important part of a *community* is its people.

"There are many more things a community needs," Mrs. Roberts went on. "It needs a post office, a bank, and places for people to pray."

At the meeting, the people talked. The list grew longer, Mrs. Roberts said. Most important of all, the new town would need a government building. It would have a meeting hall and rooms for leaders. Many people would be elected to help run the town. People living in the town would choose the leaders they wanted. They would vote for them to run the government.

"Then," Mrs. Roberts said, "Daddy brought up a good point."

"What will we name our new community?" he asked.

Water is brought to houses in pipes that start at a pumping station.

Everyone thought a long time, Mrs. Roberts reported. Then everyone talked about names. After a while, they agreed. They would call the new community Waterton.

"That's a good name," said the chairperson. "After all, water will be very important to our new town."

Do You Know?

1. How did people at the mobile home park begin the new town?
2. What do you call the person in charge of a meeting?
3. What are some things a town needs?
4. How do people become part of the government?

To Help You Learn

Using New Words

chairperson plains
reservation

Answer each question below by using one of the words above.

1. Who runs a meeting?
2. What are flat stretches of land called?
3. What is the name for land on which Indian tribes live?

Talking It Over

1. How is living in the desert different from living in other places the Robertses have visited?
2. Can the desert be changed? How?
3. Why is it important to plan a community before building it?
4. What things would you like about being a pioneer? What things would you not like?

2

Early Communities of the Desert

Matt and Lisa were drawing pictures in the sand. It was early in the morning. Soon, the sun would heat the desert. But now, the air was cool. The sound of a motor broke the silence.

"I wonder who that can be?" Lisa said. Just then, Matt saw a truck coming up the road. "Look! It's Mr. Chee."

Matt and Lisa ran to meet him. Mrs. Roberts came out of their home. They walked over to the truck to talk to Mr. Chee.

Trucks are important on big *reservations.*

"Hi," Mr. Chee said. "This is my day off. I'm going to the Navajo reservation. Would you like to come and meet my family?"

"We'd love to," Mrs. Roberts answered. "We were planning to have a picnic today. Will you and your mother join us, after our visit?"

"Thank you," answered Mr. Chee. "I would enjoy that. Please ask my mother."

"Mr. Roberts would like to come along to the reservation also," Mrs. Roberts said. "He needs more workers for the dam. Perhaps some of the people from the reservation would want to work on it."

They got into the truck. Mr. Chee stopped at the dam to pick up Mr. Roberts. Then they drove to the Navajo reservation.

This Navajo man loves his land. He lives on the Navajo *reservation.*

The Navajo Reservation

The Navajo reservation is larger than all of New England. It spreads into three states. Most of it is in Arizona. Parts cross into Utah (**ū** tä) and New Mexico. The Roberts family would see only one part of the reservation.

They looked out the window as they went. Tumbleweeds seemed to dance across the desert. Tumbleweeds are plants broken from their roots and blown by the wind. The sun shone on flat-topped mountains that looked purple and gold. Patches of grass dotted the dry hills. Twisted piñon (**pin** yōn) trees also grew there. A piñon tree is a small desert tree with seeds that can be eaten. The Navajos pick the delicious piñon nuts to eat and sell.

These two Navajos herd their sheep on horseback.

The Navajos call themselves The People. The reservation has always been their land. It is now their reservation. On it, they raise corn, beans, and squash.

Billy Chee said the Navajos are the largest American Indian tribe. They call their reservation "Dinetah." That means "Land of The People."

The Navajo have a story about when they were first created, Mr. Chee told them. He said, "A magical (**maj** ə kal) being called Changing Woman told us we should live here. Then another magical being came to us. He was First Man. First Man built four magic mountains. They were to protect Dinetah. You can see two of the magic mountains from here."

Mr. Chee pointed to the north. Lisa could see a mountain peak. It looked very close. "White people call that Mount Hesperus," Mr. Chee said. "It guards our land from the north." He pointed southeast. "That peak is called Mount Taylor by whites. We call it Turquoise (**tur** koiz) Mountain. A spirit we call Blue Flint Girl lives there. She guards us from the south."

"That mountain looks close," said Lisa. "Could we climb it?"

Mr. Chee smiled. "It looks close because the air is so clear. It is more than 70 miles away."

Billy Chee drove down the dusty road. The family saw that beans had been planted next to corn plants. As they grew, the bean vines wound themselves around the tall cornstalks.

Water flows through an *irrigation* ditch. Crops need the water.

Ditches had been dug from a stream to the field. The ditches carried water to irrigate the crops. But the stream was almost dry now. There was not much water in the ditches. In the spring, the snow melts in the mountains. This takes about 30 days. Then water runs down the rivers and into the ditches.

During the summer, the stream starts to dry up. Sometimes the crops die because there is no water. The Navajos grow food only for themselves. There is not enough water to grow food to sell.

What The People do sell is wool from their sheep. That helps the Navajos earn money for what they need to buy. Sheep are also important to the Navajos for food. The Navajos didn't always have sheep. Sheep, along with horses, were brought by the Spanish people to the Southwest about 400 years ago.

Some Navajo *hogans* look like this.
Their sides are made of wood.

In summer, the sheep are taken up to the *mesa* (**mā** sə) for grass. A mesa is a high flat place. Its name is the Spanish word for "table." The People build summer *hogans* (**hō** gənz) on the mesa and stay there until the fall. A hogan is a Navajo house. Summer hogans are made of poles and brush. Nearby are *corrals* (kə **ralz**) for the sheep. A corral is a pen in which animals are kept.

Do You Know?

1. What do the Navajos call their reservation? What does the word mean?
2. What kind of animals do the Navajos raise? Who brought these animals to the Southwest?
3. What is a Navajo house called?

Indians come to buy and sell things
at the *trading post.*

The Trading Post

Near the desert road, Lisa saw a small building.

"What's that?" she asked.

"It's a *trading post*," Mr. Chee said. "Long ago, my people didn't use money. When they needed something, they gave something else for it. This kind of buying without money is called trading. The things that are traded are called trade goods. The store is called a trading post. Today, things are still traded. But most things are bought with money."

Billy Chee told her more about trading posts.

"The trading post changed the Navajos in other ways," he said. "Before the trading post came, Navajo names were very different.

"A Navajo child was given a secret name by his or her family. No one else knew it. The child was called

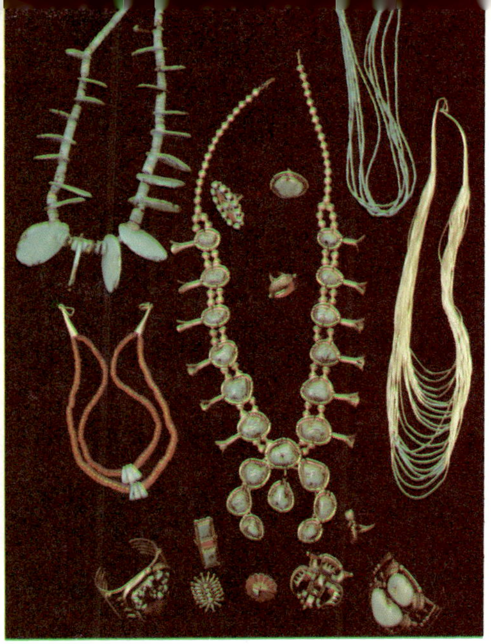

Some Navajos trade beautiful
jewelry for other goods.

by a nickname. The nickname changed as the person changed.

"When my grandfather was a child," Mr. Chee said, "he was called Loud Boy. Then he was called Tall Boy. When he grew up, he was called Talking Man. When he was old, he became Gray Man.

"At the trading post, white people did not like names that changed. Today, Navajos have one name they use all their lives."

"Oh," said Lisa. "I wish I had a secret name! But how did the trading post get started, Mr. Chee? Can you explain that for us?"

"Over a hundred years ago, the first trader came to the reservation," he said. "Soon after, more traders came. The People had wool, sheep skins, rugs, and blankets to trade. They also had jewelry made from silver and *turquoise*. Turquoise is a sky-blue or greenish-blue stone. The People got beans and sugar for their trade goods. Trading posts became places where The People could meet. Many Navajos came from far away and stayed for days.

"The traders showed the beautiful blankets and jewelry to others. People all over the country learned about Navajo art from the traders. Today, the Navajos still make, trade, and sell blankets and jewelry. They still get things from the trading post. The men get their shirts and blue jeans there. The women get velvet blouses and calico (**kal** ə kō) skirts. Calico is cotton cloth printed with colored patterns. The trading post is a busy place."

Making jewelry is an art. This man is using *turquoise* and silver.

The Hogan

As Mr. Chee drove farther, the family saw some Navajo houses. Mr. Chee stopped.

"We're here," he said.

Mr. Chee's mother's house had six sides. It was made of short logs that had been cut on each side. The logs were no longer round. They were square. The spaces between the logs had been filled with mud. The roof of the house was round and covered with earth. It had a hole in the center for smoke to escape.

Matt looked around. Some hogans had windows, but most didn't. Some had doors and others just had openings. All the doors and openings faced east. That is so The People can greet the morning sun.

There is a rug on the loom outside this *hogan.*

Navajo artists make stone carving, *pottery,* and *turquoise* jewelry.

Most people were still in their summer houses on the mesa. But Billy Chee's mother was here. She was weaving a blanket on her loom. She wove designs of squares, diamonds, circles, and flowers. Mr. Chee spoke to her in the language of The People. He explained why he had brought visitors.

"These friends have come to visit."

"They are welcome here," she said. Then she turned to the family and said in English, "Please come inside and sit down."

They followed her into the hogan. In the center of the large room was a black iron stove. A pipe from it went up to the smoke hole in the roof. Some hogans don't have stoves. Then the women cook the old way. They make a fire on the earth floor.

Navajo women weave rugs on large looms. They make colorful designs.

Around the walls were rolls of sheep skins. Everyone sat on them and leaned back against the walls. At night, the skins are unrolled and used for beds. It was comfortable inside the hogan.

Old Ways, New Ways

Mr. Chee's young sister Nita came into the hogan. She was wearing rings, bracelets, necklaces, and earrings of silver and turquoise. Mr. Chee's mother also wore a lot of jewelry.

"You have beautiful jewelry," Mrs. Roberts said.

"We wear it because turquoise is the color of the sky," Nita said. "The sky gives us the sun, the moon, and the stars at night. Wearing turquoise is an old Navajo *custom* (**kus** təm)."

Customs are the ways that people in a community do things. The Navajos have many old customs. Going to a singer is one of them. Singers heal the sick in ways learned long ago. "Heal" means to make well. Each winter, there is a *ceremony* (**ser** ə **mō** nē) nine days long. A ceremony is a special way things are done on special occasions. This nine-day ceremony is the ceremony for healing. A singer makes a sandpainting and chants prayers. Everyone thinks good thoughts. They believe this will help make the sick become well. There are dances and songs. It is a time for The People to be together.

Sandpainting is an old Navajo *custom*. It is also an art.

Not all Navajos go to singers when they are ill. Some go to doctors. Some go to both. There are old ways and new ways to do things. The People want to keep their old customs. They want to be close to the land. They want to speak their own language. But they want new things, too. They know some new things, like the dam, will help The People. That is why many of the Navajos wanted to work on the dam.

Very soon it was time to go. Mrs. Roberts took pictures of Mr. Chee's family. Nita took a picture of the Roberts family. Then Mrs. Roberts asked, "Mrs. Chee and Nita, will you join us for a picnic?" Mrs. Chee was too busy to come. But Nita said yes. She said a picnic would be lots of fun.

Do You Know?

1. What is a trading post?
2. What name do the Navajos call themselves?
3. What are some old ways and some new ways that Navajos do things?

Things To Do

1. Think up a secret name for yourself. What nicknames would you use?
2. Draw a hogan. Label its parts.

Indian Pottery

At the mobile home park, all the children were busy. They were getting ready for school. Matt and Lisa were glad that school was starting. They would learn new things. They would meet new friends. They didn't have far to walk. A small school had been built at the park.

Most of the children had come to New Mexico for the first time. There was much to learn about their new home.

"Who were the first people to farm in the Southwest?" Lisa asked her teacher on the first day.

Mr. Berg told the class about some of the first people. They were the Basket Makers. They lived in the Southwest 2,000 years ago. In one way, they were like Woodland Indians and Navajos. They met

This kind of Indian *pottery* was made long ago by Pueblo Indians.

all their needs from the land around them. At first, these people built their homes in pits. Then they built their homes in high *cliffs* (**klifs**). A cliff is a steep wall of rock or earth. The cliffs kept the Basket Makers safe from their enemies.

The Basket Makers made tightly woven baskets. Some held water. They covered the inside of the baskets with *clay* (**klā**). Clay is a kind of earth. The clay kept the water from dripping out.

Then one day, the Basket Makers learned how to do something new. They learned how to make *pottery* (**pot** ə rē). Pottery is bowls, pots, and other dishes made of clay.

No one knows for sure how the Basket Makers discovered how to make pottery. Maybe someone left a clay-lined basket near a fire. After many hours, the

These dancers are balancing hand-painted *pottery* on their heads.

basket had burned away. But the clay had become hard from the heat of the fire. It was a clay pot!

Today, the Pueblo (**pweb** lō) Indians are famous for their pottery. The Basket Makers were the ancestors of the Pueblo Indians.

"Do you have any pottery to show us?" Lisa asked.

"No," Mr. Berg answered. "But I have an idea. We can visit a *pueblo* to see pottery being made. Our class can go on a field trip. But first, let's talk about what a pueblo is."

What Is a Pueblo?

" 'Pueblo' is the Spanish word for village," Mr. Berg said. "So a pueblo is a community. The Indians who live in pueblos are called Pueblo Indians. There are 19 pueblos in New Mexico. And there are four pueblo languages. But Pueblo Indians of different villages do many things the same way. They all build *adobe* (ə **dō** bē) houses.

Adobe is made from clay. The clay is mixed with water and becomes a thick mud. Then the mud is mixed with straw to make it strong. It is shaped into bricks. The bricks are baked in the sun. When they are hard, they are used to build a house."

Mr. Berg showed the class some pictures of pueblos.

Some *pueblos* have kept the old Indian ways of life.

"There are two kinds of houses," he said. "One kind was built in pueblos long ago. The other kind is built in the pueblos of today.

"The older houses were built like apartment buildings. Each building had four or five floors. Each floor had one room less than the floor below. To get inside, people climbed ladders. These ladders were placed against outside walls. The people went into their rooms from openings in the flat roofs.

"Each apartment was the same size. And they were all alike inside. That's because the Pueblo Indians

The Taos *pueblo* is very old. People use ladders to climb in and out.

believe that everyone is equal. They believe that everyone should live the same way. Houses in the newer pueblos are separate, but still made of adobe."

"Do people still live in the old pueblos?" Lisa's classmate Joe asked.

"Yes," Mr. Berg said. "Some Indians want to live close to nature. They want to live without things that are made by machines. The pueblo in Taos (**tous**), New Mexico, has no electricity or running water. Some Taos Indians don't want water piped in. They don't want electric lights or stoves. They want to live as their ancestors did."

"We would like to see a pueblo," Rosa, another of Lisa's classmates, said. "When can we go?"

"Soon," Mr. Berg said. "Very soon."

Do You Know?

1. How do we think the Basket Makers learned to make pottery?
2. Where did the Basket Makers build their homes?
3. From what do Pueblo Indians build their houses?

Things To Do

1. Read an Indian story. Tell it to your classmates.
2. Start a picture album of Navajo and Pueblo life.

Visiting a Pueblo

Mr. Berg took the class to a modern pueblo. Its houses had electricity and running water. A good road went there. Some of the Pueblo Indians owned cars. They drove to work outside the pueblo. But their families lived on the reservation.

When the class arrived, Mr. Berg spoke to the *governor* (**guv** ər nər). The people of the pueblo vote for their governor. He is in charge of running the village.

Many pueblos have two leaders. One is the governor. The other is a religious leader. The people choose him, also. His job is to help people keep their old customs. It is not always easy. New things such as TV have come to some pueblos. New things can

No one lives in this old *pueblo* now.
It was built hundreds of years ago.

change old ways. The religious leader must think over what new things his people might have. He has a few men to help him. Together, they make the rules.

The Pueblo Indians have had many of the same customs since the time of the Basket Makers. Their customs include the Corn Dance and the Snake Dance. Following customs helps the Pueblo Indians stay together. Following the rules of the tribe also helps them stay together.

Mr. Berg told the class, "We also must follow the rules of the pueblo. The governor says we may not go into the *kiva* (**kē** və). We may only look at it from the outside."

"What's a kiva?" someone asked.

Pueblo Indians have many *customs* such as dancing together.

Part of the *kiva* is above the ground.
Men meet in the underground room.

The governor showed the class a round house in the center of the village. Part of the kiva was underground. Only Indian men, he said, are allowed to go there. They enter the kiva through a hole in the roof. Women and outsiders may not go in. When Indian boys are old enough, they go to the kiva. It is like a secret club room. Its walls are painted with designs in red, white, green, and yellow. There, the boys are taught the customs of their people. They learn the old stories and the old prayers. They are taught special dances. In the kiva, the boys learn Pueblo ways.

Corn is an important Indian *crop.* A girl is dressed for a corn dance.

Work in a Pueblo

Mr. Berg talked more about life in a pueblo.

"Everybody in the pueblo has special jobs to do," he said. "There are no fights over who does what. The Pueblo Indians follow the rules."

The men, he explained, do the farming. Their most important crop is corn. The men also hunt and care for the animals.

The women build most of the houses. They always own the family house. They own everything inside the house as well. Many times the children have the mother's last name, not the father's. The women also make pottery and prepare food.

Mr. Berg's class watched a woman bake bread. First, she turned the corn into meal. She did this by grinding it between rough stones. Then she mixed the dough. Finally, she put the dough into an outdoor oven. The oven looked like a beehive. Long ago, women used these ovens every day. Now, many Pueblo Indians have stoves in their homes. But they still like to bake in the ovens.

Other Pueblo Customs

The class went on to another part of the pueblo. Women were baking clay pots over a hot fire. Each pueblo makes its own kind of pottery. The pottery of each pueblo has a special shape or color. And the

Children wear special clothing for *celebrations.*

pottery of each pueblo has its own designs. The designs tell you in which village the pottery was made.

Some things about each pueblo are different. But many things are the same. The children in each pueblo speak their own language at home. But they all speak English in school. Pueblo children wear clothes from a store when they go to school. But they also have specially-made clothing. They use it for their dances and other celebrations.

The oldest Pueblo custom is friendship. Pueblo Indians live in friendship among themselves and others. Long ago, the Navajos and the Pueblo Indians were enemies. Now, they are good neighbors. The Pueblo Indians taught the Navajos how to farm in the dry desert. The Navajos taught the Pueblo Indians how to make silver jewelry.

The *pueblo* is a peaceful place.
Indians live there in friendship.

Indian children of today sometimes dress like children of long ago.

"People can learn from each other," Mr. Berg said.

"Yes," said Lisa. "And I learned a lot today from our visit to the pueblo."

Do You Know?

1. What are some Pueblo Indian customs? Are they different from Navajo customs?
2. What jobs do Pueblo Indian men do?
3. What jobs do Pueblo Indian women do?
4. What did the Pueblo Indians and the Navajos teach each other?

To Help You Learn

Using New Words

mesa	turquoise	cliff
hogan	pottery	clay
corral	custom	trading post
ceremony	pueblo	kiva
adobe	governor	

Do you remember the meanings of the words listed above?

Find each word in the chapter you have just read. Read the sentence in which each is first used. Make up your own sentence for each word.

Talking It Over

1. How are the Navajos like the Pueblo Indians? How are they different?
2. How do the Navajos use the land around them to help meet their needs?
3. Could the Pueblo Indians live the same way if they lived in the eastern woodlands? Explain your answer.
4. Why might some Indians want to keep some of their old customs? Why might they want to do some things in new ways?

3

A Community Grows

Lisa, Matt, and Mr. Roberts stood at the front door of their house. Mrs. Roberts took their picture many times.

"Smile," she said. "Say 'cheese.' "

"Oh, Lee," said Mr. Roberts. "I'd rather eat than pose for pictures. Isn't it time for our special celebration cake?"

They went inside their ranch house. There, on the table, was a chocolate cake. Mr. Roberts lit three candles.

DONALD GATES

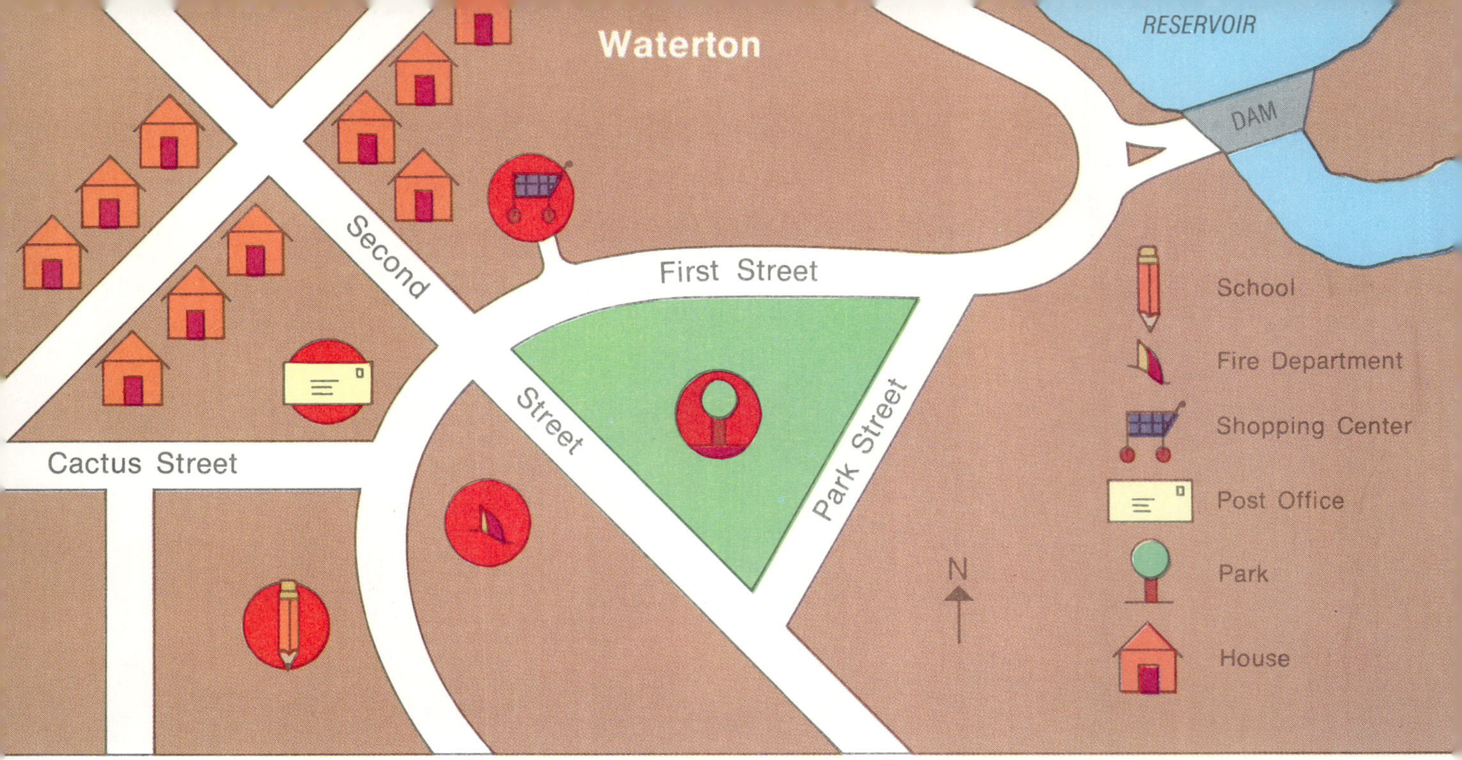

"Three years ago today!" he said. "Exactly three years ago we arrived at the mobile home park. And now the time has come to return to Elmville."

They looked out the window. Houses now lined the streets. Grass, plants, and flowers grew in every yard. But these were not the only changes.

Lisa was tall and thin. She was eleven years old. In a few weeks she would begin sixth grade. Matt, at nine, was ready for fourth grade.

Mrs. Roberts sighed. Then she said, "A lot has happened in three years. Let's think about the changes in our life."

The most important part of a *community* is its people.

The Reservoir

"I'll begin," Mr. Roberts said. "I think the most important change for all of us has been the dam. If we hadn't built the dam, none of us would be here.

"The earth wall of the dam was built a long time ago. It was built across a *canyon*. A canyon, you remember, is a valley with high, steep sides. A river flows down the canyon.

"Each spring, when the snow melted, more water came down the river. But the walls of the dam kept the river from flowing farther down the canyon. The canyon behind the dam is filling. It is becoming a large

A dam's *reservoir* is a sort of water bank.

lake. It is called a *reservoir* (**rez** ər vwär). A reservoir is a place where water for a community is stored. The water stays there until it is needed."

"Oh, Daddy!" said Lisa. "You and your reservoir! That reservoir is our beautiful lake. When we first came here, all we could see were rocks, cliffs, and canyons. Now we can swim and water ski. How can you call our lake a reservoir?"

Mr. Roberts laughed. "Because that's what it is, honey," he said. "Dams and reservoirs may not sound exciting. But just think what your life here would be without them."

"No electric lights," said Mrs. Roberts.

"No television," said Matt.

Machines inside *hydroelectric plants* produce electricity from water.

"No stoves," said Lisa. "And no refrigerators. No washing machines. No vacuum cleaners."

Mr. Roberts went on. "We have all those things because of the *hydroelectric* (**hī** drō i **lek** trik) *plant*. A hydroelectric plant makes electricity from water power. Water flowing from the dam turns machines inside the plant. And the machines make electricity. They bring electricity to our desert town."

Desert Farms

"There have been a lot of changes," Lisa said. "Waterton really changed when the big farms started. More people have come. The school has gotten bigger."

"You can thank the dam again," Mr. Roberts said. "Without it, that farmland would still be desert. The dam has made it possible to irrigate the land."

"I don't understand," said Lisa. "I know the Pueblo Indians and Navajos used irrigation for years. Why couldn't they grow larger crops?"

"Because they did not have a reservoir, Lisa," said Mr. Roberts. "Sometimes there was too much water in the river. Then there would be a flood. Sometimes there was too little water. Then there would be a *drought* (**drout**). A drought is a long time without water. Crops can die during a drought.

Water is used to *irrigate* dry land.
Nothing grows without water.

"The dam changed all that. The water needed for irrigation is stored in the reservoir. Water is let out where and when it is needed. The water gets to the fields through irrigation ditches. Or it comes to the fields through pipes. Now we can grow lots of fruits and vegetables around here. The desert has become a garden."

A Recreation Community

"The lake has also changed," said Mrs. Roberts.

"Remember when it was new?" asked Matt. "Lisa and I used to bike there after school. Only a few of us

This *reservoir* is also a lake. It is used for swimming and boating.

kids played there then. After the hot ride, the cool water felt great. It was fun to swim in the middle of the desert."

"People heard about the swimming and the good fishing," put in Mrs. Roberts. "Now they come to swim and fish in the reservoir. This year Waterton built the campground and a better road to the lake. People in campers are spending their vacations here. Now, many people use the lake."

"And," added Lisa. "There's a motel near the lake. And a new restaurant. Our lake has become a business."

"That's right," said Mrs. Roberts. "It's the *recreation* (rek rē ā shən) business. People are willing to pay to relax and enjoy themselves."

Do You Know?

1. What is a reservoir?
2. How can a hydroelectric plant help a community?
3. How can a reservoir help desert farms?

Things To Do

1. Who are the leaders of your community? Make a list of their names and jobs.
2. Find pictures of special communities for a class bulletin board.

These *retired* people enjoy golf.

A Retirement Community

"Can we think of any other ways in which Waterton has changed?" asked Mr. Roberts.

"What about Sunshine Village?" asked Lisa. "Why did the people at Sunshine Village come here?"

"Many of the people at Sunshine Village worked hard all their lives," Mrs. Roberts said. "Now they are not young anymore. They have *retired* (ri **tīrd**) from their jobs. Retired means they do not work at those jobs any more. Many older people, and many retired people, want a warm place to live. They want a place where they can spend time outdoors.

"I guess we can thank the *climate* (**klī** mət) for our retirement community," said Mr. Roberts. "Waterton's climate is hot and dry."

The Southwest Today

Find pictures on these pages that show where people live, work, and play in the Southwest. Which buildings show old ways of life? Which buildings show that the Southwest today is busy and growing?

How can you be in four states at the same time? It's easy if you visit a place in the Southwest called the Four Corners. The girl is lying where Arizona, Colorado, New Mexico, and Utah meet.

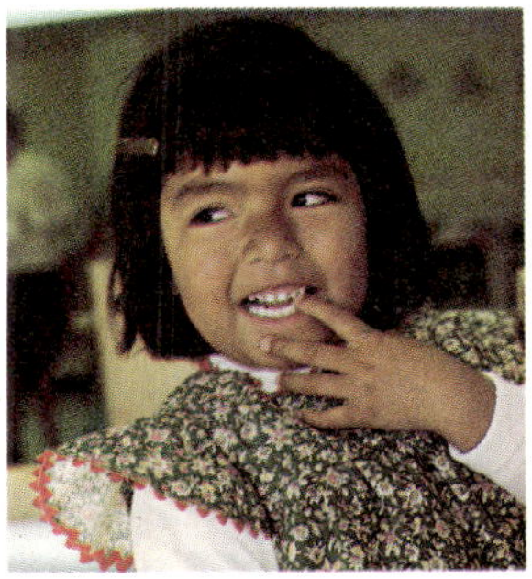

LAMBS

La Fonda
PARKING

Working in the Southwest

People in the Southwest make a living in many different ways. How many kinds of work do you see? How does a dam make some of this work possible?

Which pictures show jobs that use the land? Which pictures show jobs done by machines? Which pictures show jobs done by hand?

21

PETROLANE

Thinking About the Future

It had grown late. The Robertses moved outdoors to the patio. The stars twinkled brightly in the clear desert air.

"My favorite time of day," said Mrs. Roberts. "Time to stop and think about the future."

The *future* (**fū** chər) is anything that will happen after this very moment.

"I hope this town does not become too big," said Mr. Roberts.

"Why, Dad?" asked Matt. "Why can't it keep growing?"

"Because the reservoir has only so much water," Mr. Roberts explained. "What if there were too many farms, houses, and businesses? They would use so much water that the reservoir wouldn't stay full. Then there wouldn't be enough water for the power plant. There wouldn't be enough water for irrigation. There wouldn't be enough water to drink."

"I didn't think of that," Matt said. "I guess Waterton shouldn't get too big."

"That's the way we have planned it," said Mr. Roberts. "We have planned for Waterton to have *limits* to its growth. A limit is when or where something must end. This community will have limits on the number of houses. It will have limits on the number of its businesses and farms, just the way we have a limit on the time we will spend here."

Working Towards the Future

"I am looking forward to returning to Vermont," said Mrs. Roberts. "But I hope Waterton will always be a nice place to live. I want it to stay beautiful. I want the air to be clean. I want people to feel safe."

"Good for you, Lee!" said Mr. Roberts. "You want this community to do more than meet basic needs. You want it to make life better for the people who live in it."

"But can we help a community do that?" asked Lisa.

Do you think these people enjoy life in their *community*? Why?

Community leaders sometimes use schoolrooms for meeting places.

"I've been thinking about that," said Mrs. Roberts. "When we get back to Elmville, I will try to be elected to the board that runs the town. If I'm elected, I'll be a community leader. I'll help decide how our community will be."

"We'll help, Mom," said Lisa. "We'll talk with people in town. We'll ask them to vote for you."

"We'll put up signs," added Matt. "The signs will say 'Elect Lee Roberts! She can do the job.' "

"Matt, Lisa," said Mr. Roberts. "What about you? What are your plans for the future?"

"Gee, Dad," said Matt. "Getting back to Elmville will be exciting. I'll see kids I used to know. And I'll meet some new ones. I'll have lots to tell."

"I haven't forgotten about becoming a page," said Lisa. "I still want to go to Washington, D.C. I'll write to our member of Congress. Maybe one of my old friends in Elmville will want to become a page, too."

"So many plans for the future," said Mrs. Roberts. "Remember when we left Elmville? We thought New Mexico would be the end of our trip. In a way it was. In another way, it was just the beginning. It was the beginning of everything that has happened since."

"And tonight," said Lisa, "is another beginning. Everything that will happen in the future begins tonight."

Do You Know?

1. How can a reservoir help make a recreation community?
2. Why have some people moved to retirement communities in the desert?
3. What might happen if Waterton became too big?

To Help You Learn

Using New Words

climate future reservoir
drought reservation

Read the new words listed above. Write a sentence to explain the meaning of each one.

Talking It Over

1. What is a recreation community? What special things can people do in this kind of community?
2. What is a retirement community? Who lives in one?

Activities: Planning a Community

You have read about how one group of people planned a community. See how you would plan one.

Where will your community be built?

What types of transportation will the people use?

Will the homes be houses or apartment buildings?

Where will people get their food and clothing? Where will they buy other things they need?

Will the community need schools? Hospitals? What places for recreation will it have?

How will the people get news? How will they govern themselves?

Draw a map of how your community will look. What will you call it? Tell why you planned it as you did.

Learning About
Maps and Globes

Maps and globes are special tools. They help us to understand our earth and the people, places, and things on it. Maps and globes are only useful tools if we know how to use them. The lessons in this section will help you improve your skills in using maps and globes. These map and globe skills will help you to understand the world around you.

Words to Watch for

border
cardinal directions
compass rose
equator
hemisphere
hills
intermediate directions
key
landforms
mountains
plains
plateaus
road maps
rotates
scale bar
vegetation

LESSON

1 Our States and Their Capitals

This map of the United States shows the 50 states and their capitals. The line or *border* drawn around a state shows where one state ends and another state or country begins. What countries and oceans border our country?

CANADA
UNITED STATES
OF AMERICA
ATLANTIC OCEAN
NORTH DAKOTA
Bismarck
SOUTH DAKOTA
NEBRASKA
Lincoln
KANSAS
Topeka
OKLAHOMA
Oklahoma City
TEXAS
Austin
MINNESOTA
St. Paul
IOWA
Des Moines
MISSOURI
Jefferson City
ARKANSAS
Little Rock
LOUISIANA
Baton Rouge
WISCONSIN
Madison
ILLINOIS
Springfield
MICHIGAN
Lansing
INDIANA
Indianapolis
OHIO
Columbus
KENTUCKY
Frankfort
TENNESSEE
Nashville
MISSISSIPPI
Jackson
ALABAMA
Montgomery
GEORGIA
Atlanta
FLORIDA
Tallahassee
SOUTH CAROLINA
Columbia
NORTH CAROLINA
Raleigh
VIRGINIA
Richmond
WEST VIRGINIA
Charleston
Washington, D.C.
MARYLAND
Annapolis
DELAWARE
Dover
NEW JERSEY
Trenton
PENNSYLVANIA
Harrisburg
NEW YORK
Albany
CONNECTICUT
Hartford
RHODE ISLAND
Providence
MASSACHUSETTS
Boston
NEW HAMPSHIRE
Concord
VERMONT
Montpelier
MAINE
Augusta
Missouri River
Mississippi River
Ohio River
CANADA
UNITED STATES
MEXICO
0 Kilometers 400
0 Miles 200

LESSON

2 How a Map Shows Directions

North, south, east, and west are the four main or *cardinal directions.* North is the direction of the North Pole. Face toward north. Your right hand now points east. Your left hand points west. Your back is toward south, the direction of the South Pole.

A *compass rose,* like the one shown on this page, can show directions on maps. It also shows the *intermediate directions* marked halfway

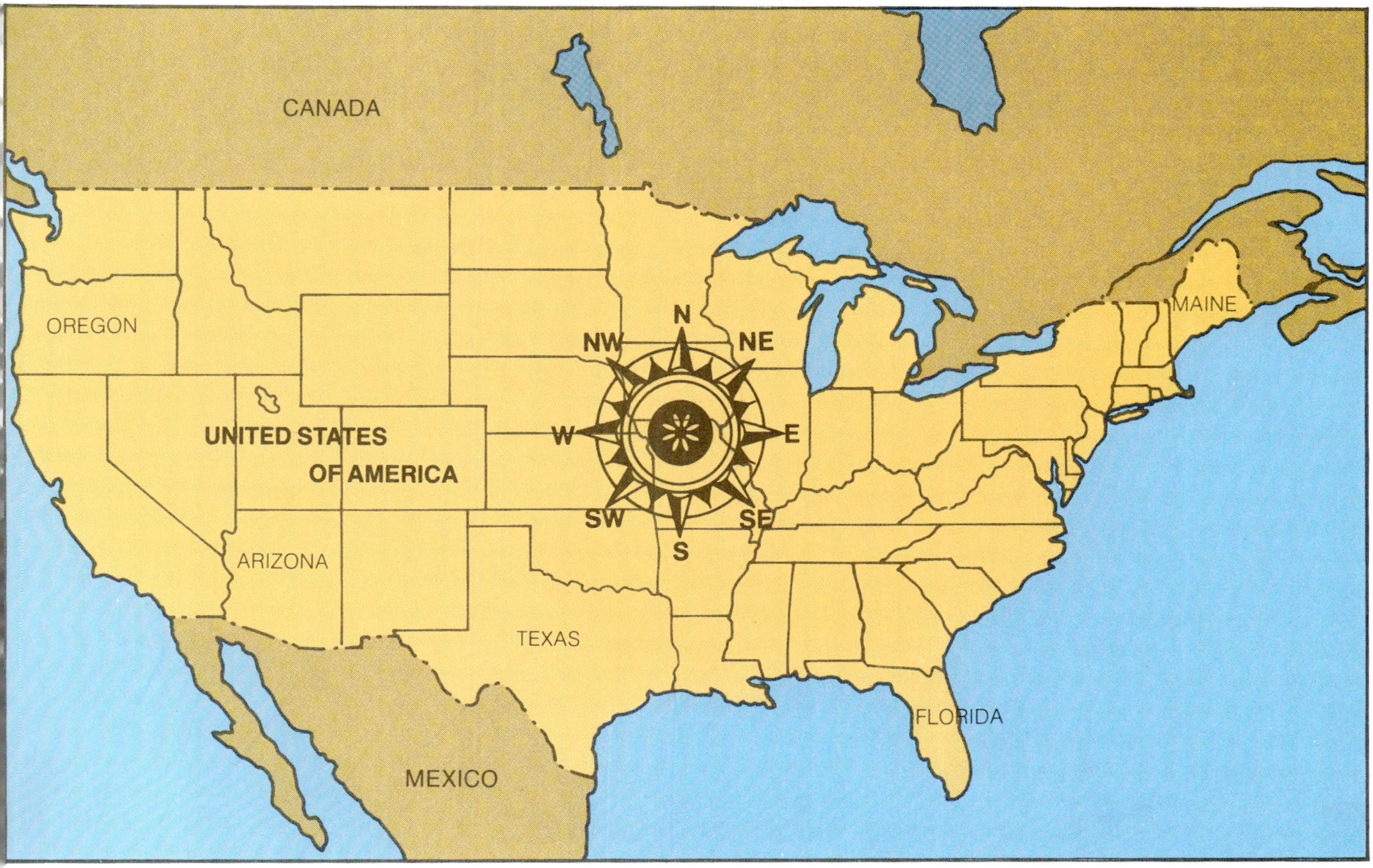

between the cardinal directions. Name the four intermediate directions.

Use the compass rose on this map of the United States to tell:

Which direction is Texas from Florida?

What country is north of the United States?

In which direction would you travel going from Maine to Arizona?

Which way would you travel to go from Oregon to your state?

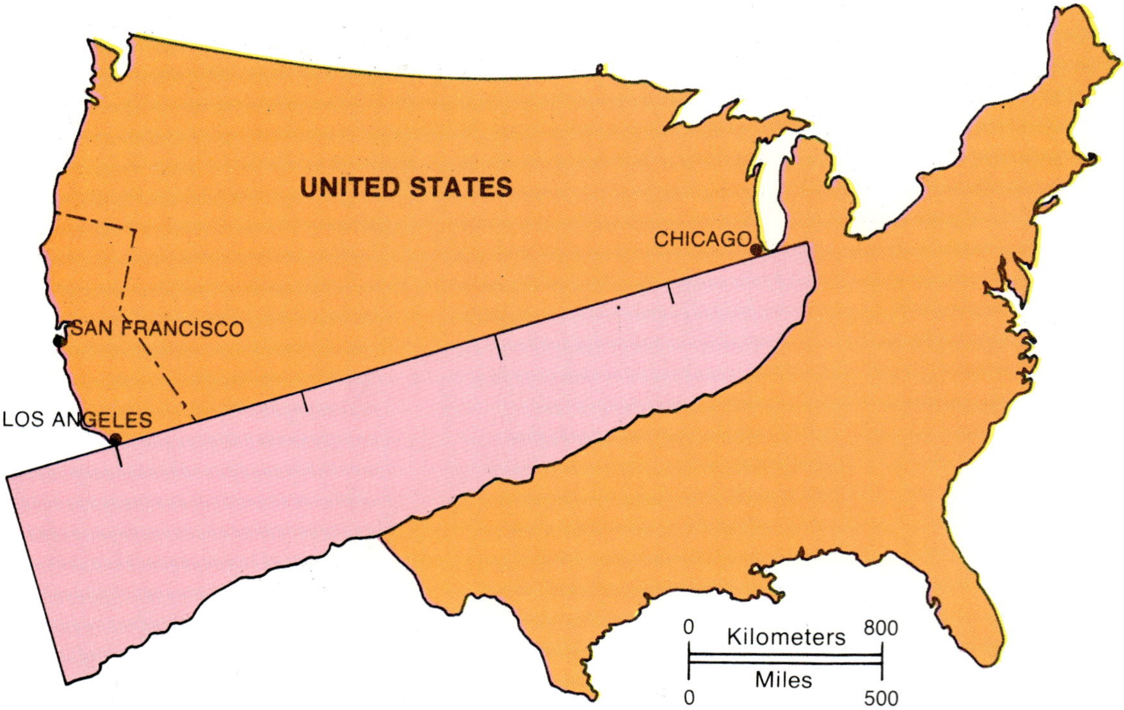

LESSON

3 Using Map Scales

The map on this page shows how to use a *scale bar.* Take a scrap of paper. Lay it against the scale bar below the map. Mark the paper with lines like those on the scale bar. Slide the paper along to copy all the marks you need. If you want to find the distance in kilometers, copy the marks on the top of the scale bar. To find the distance in miles, copy the marks on the bottom.

Now, you have made your own scale bar. Suppose that you want to find the distance between Chicago and Los Angeles. Hold your

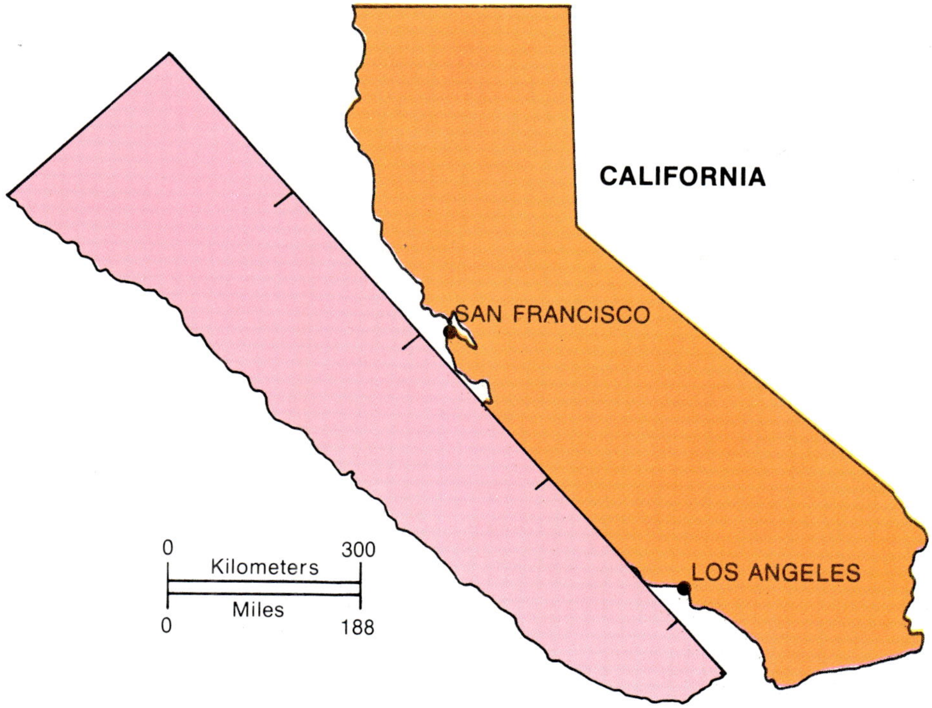

own scale bar between the two places. How far is it between the two places?

Now make your own scale bar for the map above. Find out how far it is from San Francisco to Los Angeles by using this map of California.

Your new scale bar is as long as the old one. But the marks stand for smaller distances. This is because the map of California shows a smaller part of the United States than the map on 294.

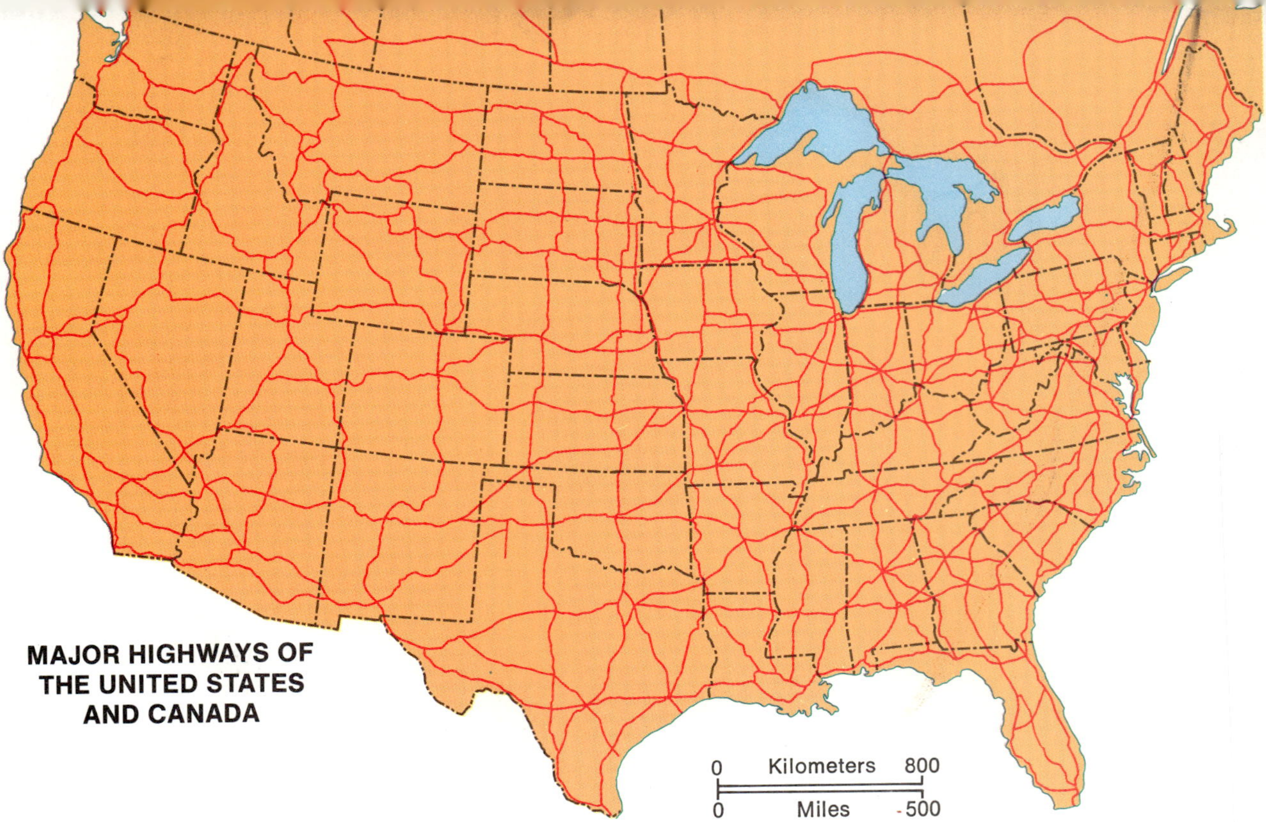

MAJOR HIGHWAYS OF THE UNITED STATES AND CANADA

LESSON

4 Understanding Road Maps

Which of these three *road maps* would help you drive to the Space Center in Houston, Texas?

If you live in a state far from Texas, the highway map of the United States will show you how to get to Texas.

If you are already in Texas, the road map of the state will help you find the way to Houston.

If you are in Houston, the map of that area will guide you to the Space Center.

All three road maps show the roads you can take. All three show the direction and the distance you need to travel.

HIGHWAYS OF TEXAS
NORTH
WEST
EAST
SOUTH
Amarillo
Lubbock
Fort Worth
Dallas
Abilene
Big Spring
El Paso
Austin
Orange
Houston
Galveston
San Antonio
Corpus Christi
Laredo
0 Kilometers 160
0 Miles 100
HOUSTON
Galena Park
Pasadena
Bellaire
Lyndon B. Johnson Space Center
0 Kilometers 15
0 Miles 10

LESSON
5 Reading a Landform Map

There are four kinds of land that cover most of the earth's land surface. They are called *landforms.* The pictures below show these landforms.

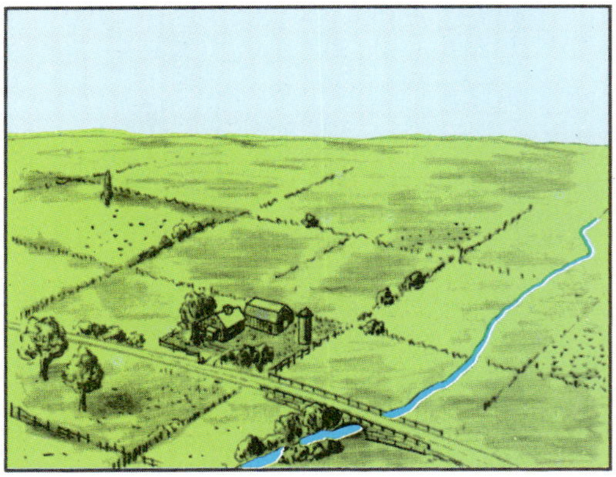

Plains are flat, or gently rolling lands.

Hills are lower than mountains.

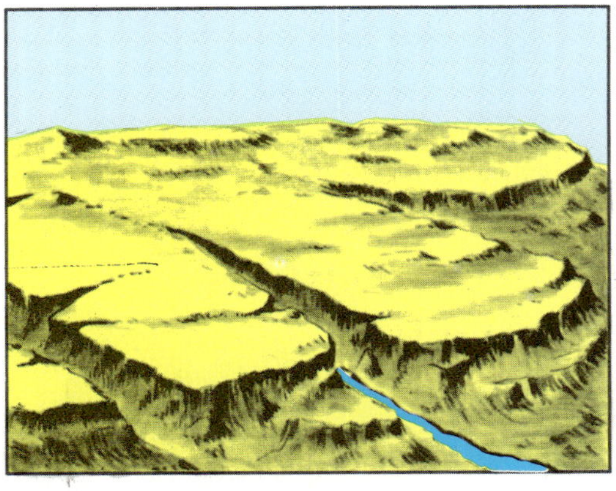

Plateaus are flat lands with steep sides that are usually higher than plains.

Mountains may rise to high peaks or points. Some mountains are part of a range or group.

LANDFORMS OF THE UNITED STATES

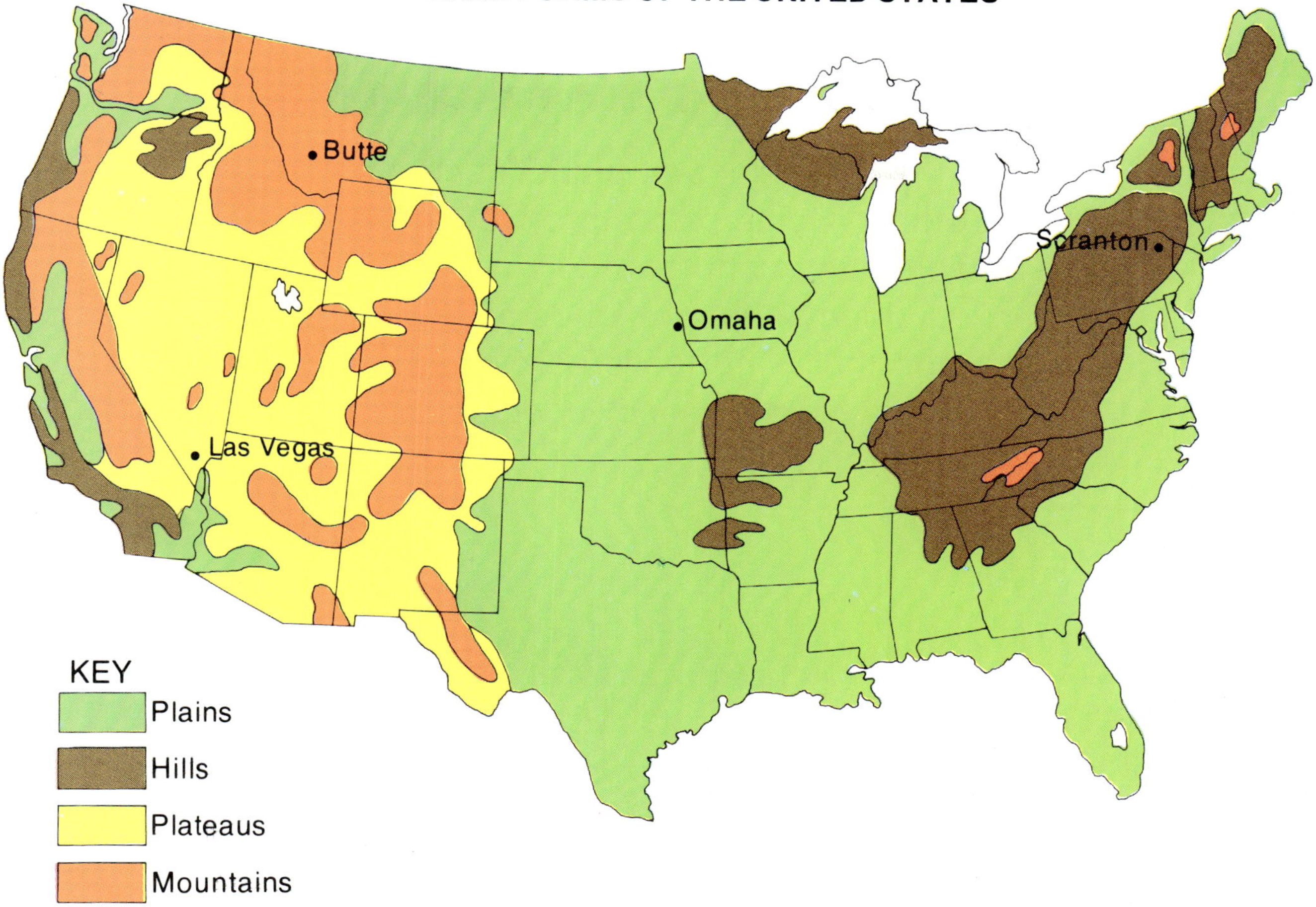

On this map, colors show the different kinds of land in the United States. Which color shows mountains on the map? Which color shows hills? Which colors tell where plains and plateaus are found?

Can you tell:

Which city is on a plain?
Which city is in the mountains?
Which city is in the hills?
Which city is on a plateau?

LESSON

6 Reading a Vegetation Map

Some kinds of plants need more water than others. Some plants grow better in one kind of soil than in another.

Many different kinds of plants grow wild on land that is not covered by farms or cities. These plants, called *vegetation,* are shown in the pictures below.

Trees cover land that gets more water than grassland.

Grassland is land covered mostly by grasses. Some rain falls on grassland.

Little or no vegetation grows on land that is too dry or too high.

Dry-land vegetation grows where there is little rain. Few plants grow on dry land.

VEGETATION IN THE UNITED STATES

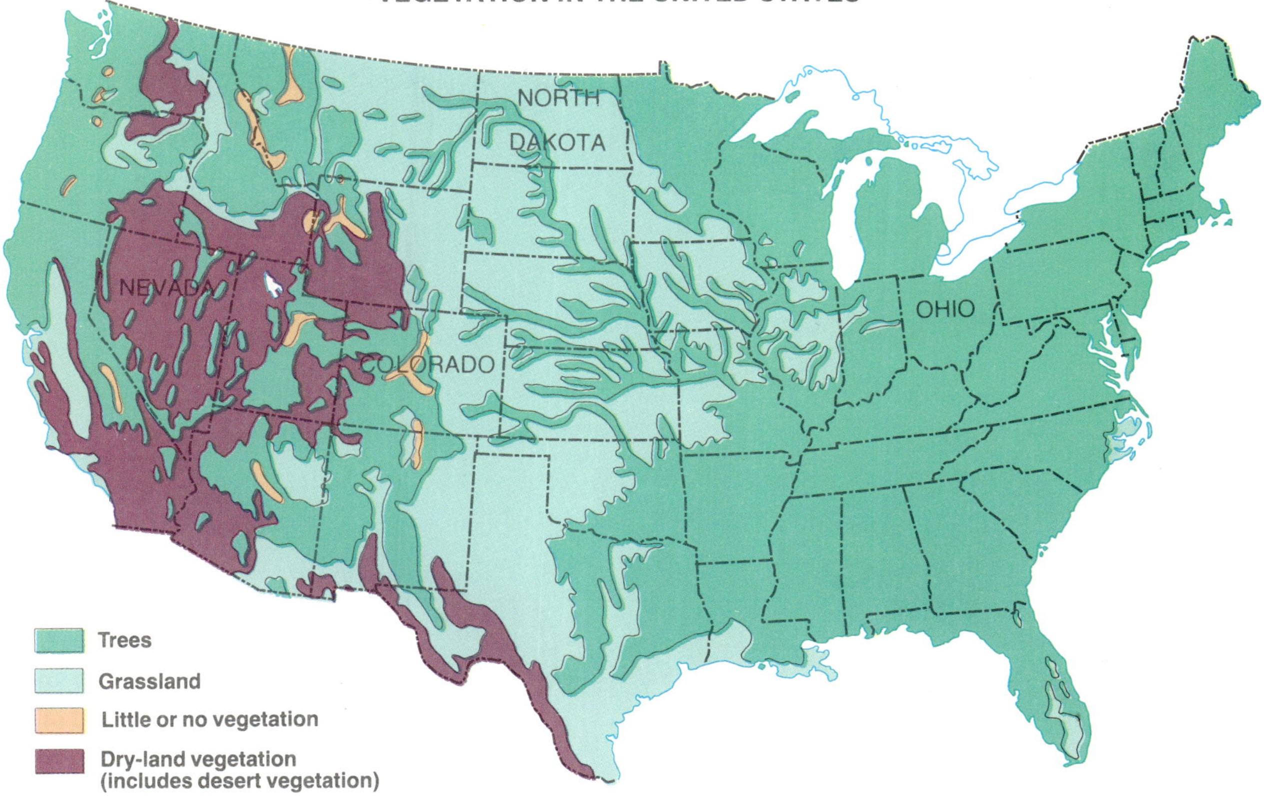

Look at the kinds of vegetation shown on this vegetation map of the United States. How is each shown? Look at the four states named on this map.

Can you tell:

Which state is covered mostly by grassland?
Which state has some land where no plants grow?
Which state is covered mostly by dry land?
Which state is covered by trees?

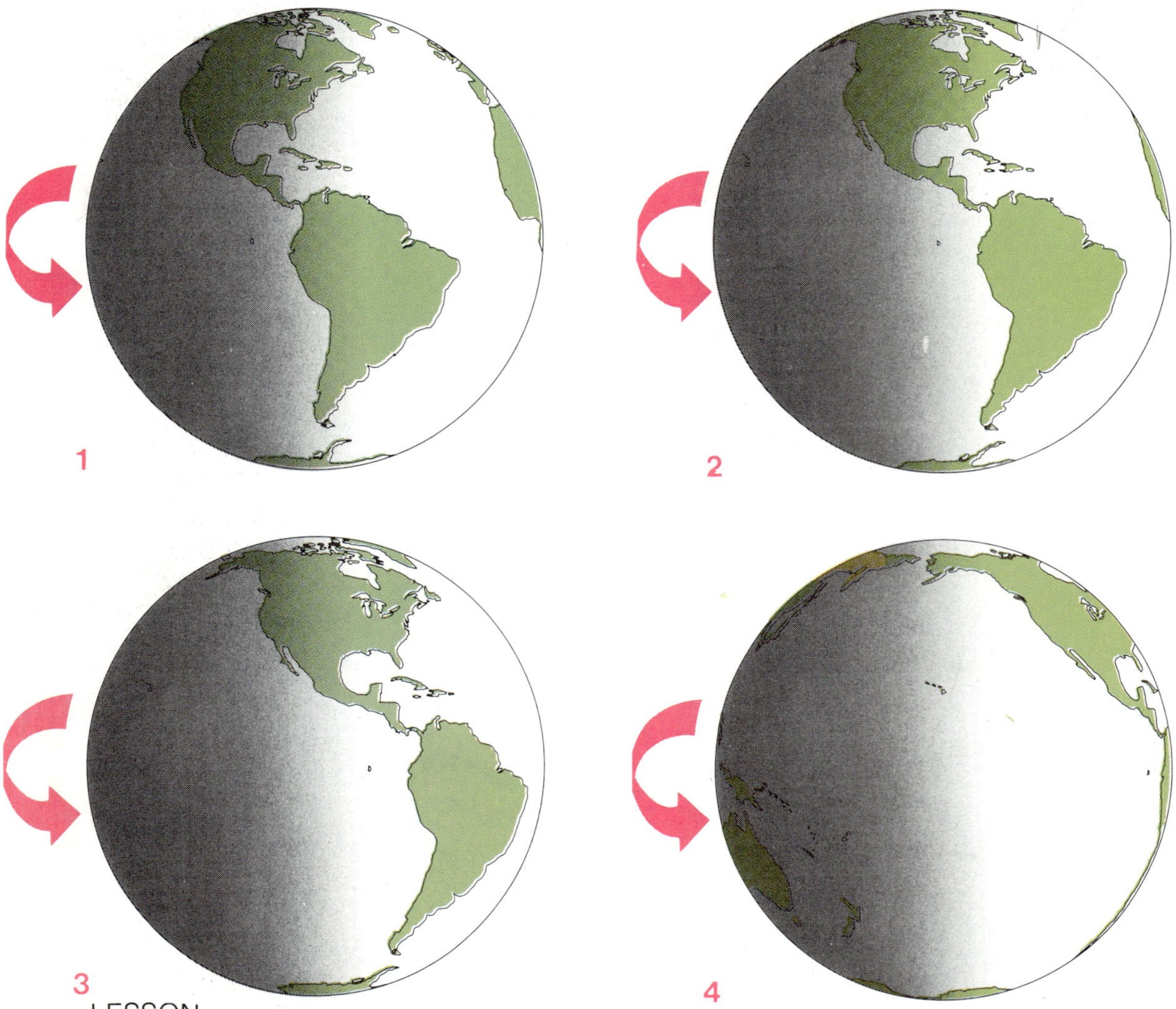

LESSON

7 Understanding Day and Night

The earth never stops turning. It always spins at the same speed from west to east. In one day and night, it turns or *rotates* (**rō** tāts) completely around.

As the earth turns, sunlight shines on one side of it. While half of the earth has daylight, the

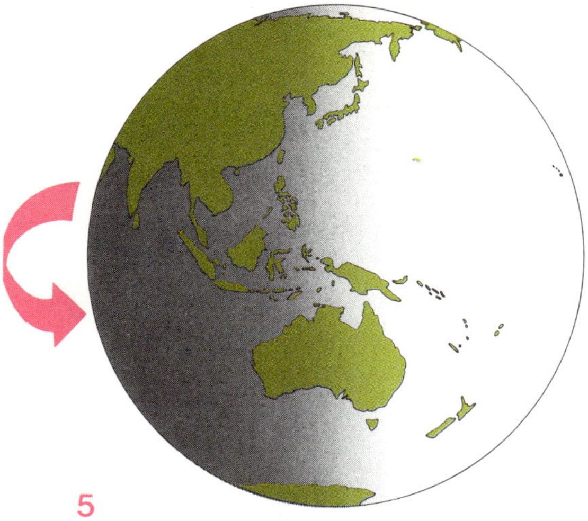

5

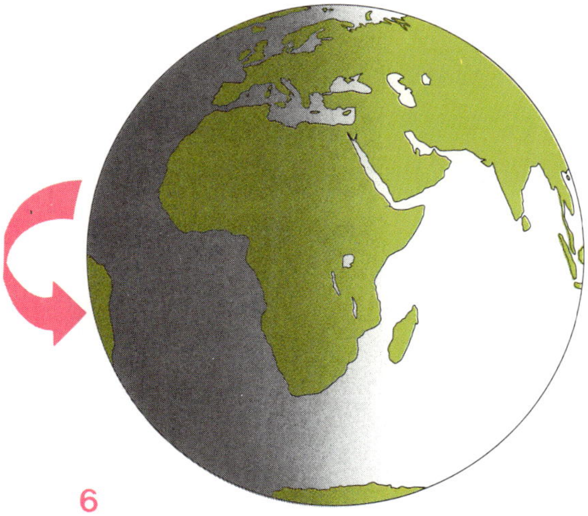

6

7

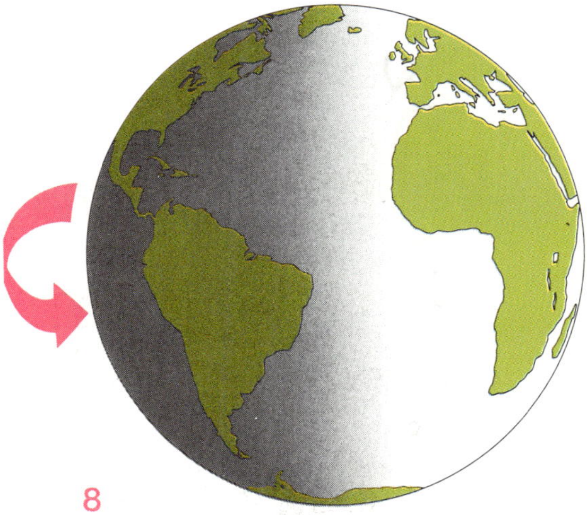

8

other half is dark. When it is day where you live, it is night on the other side of the earth.

Look at the pictures of the earth on these pages. Which pictures show part of the United States? the United States in daylight? Why doesn't the United States appear in every picture? Find the place you live. Tell if it is having day or night in each picture.

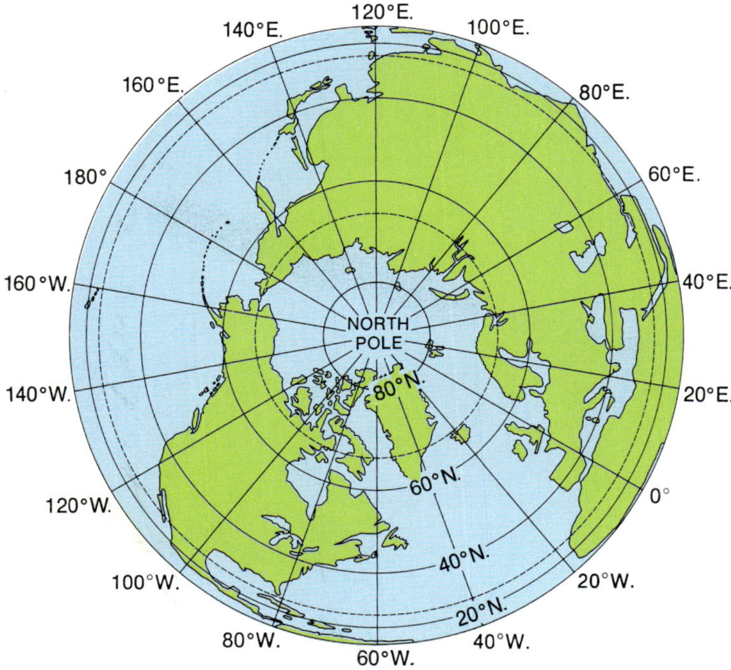

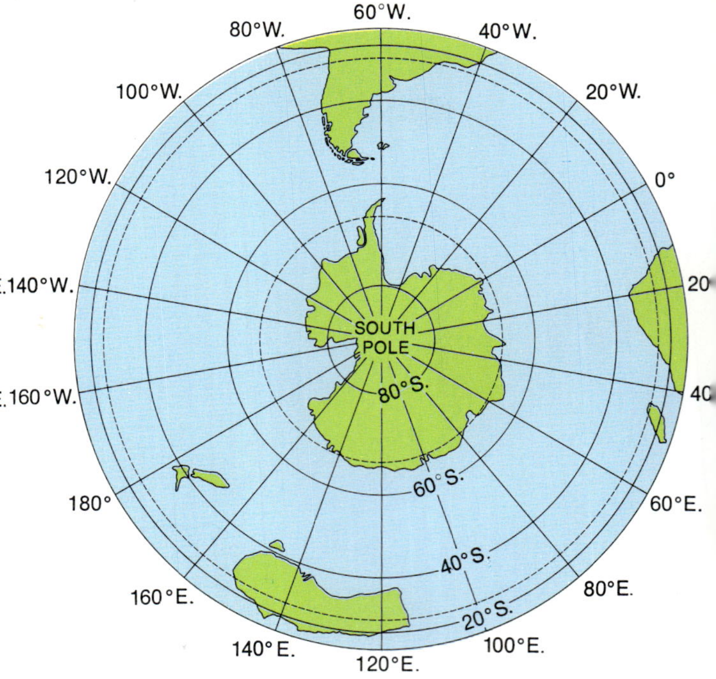

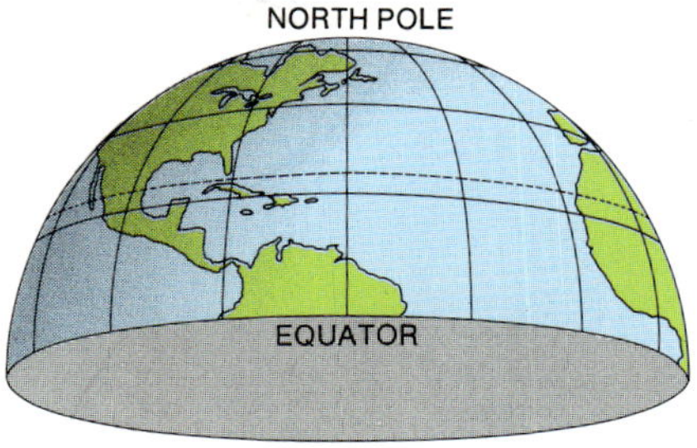

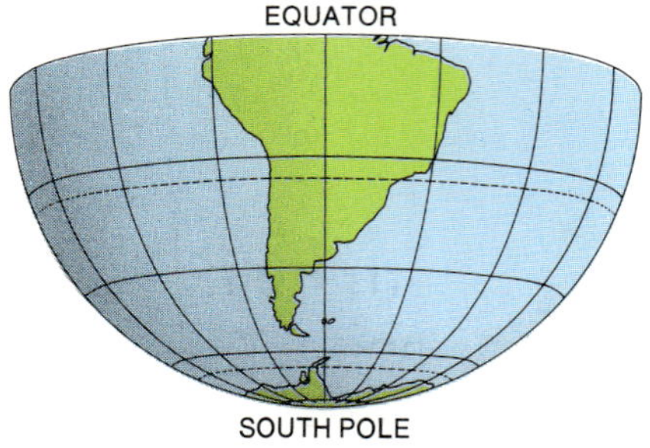

LESSON
8 Understanding Hemispheres

A globe is a model of the earth. No matter how you look, you can only see half of the globe at one time. Half of a globe is called a *hemisphere* (**hem** ə sfēr).

Look at the pictures of the globe on this page. The globe has been cut into two equal parts along a line called the *equator* (i **kwā** tər). This line is drawn around the globe halfway between

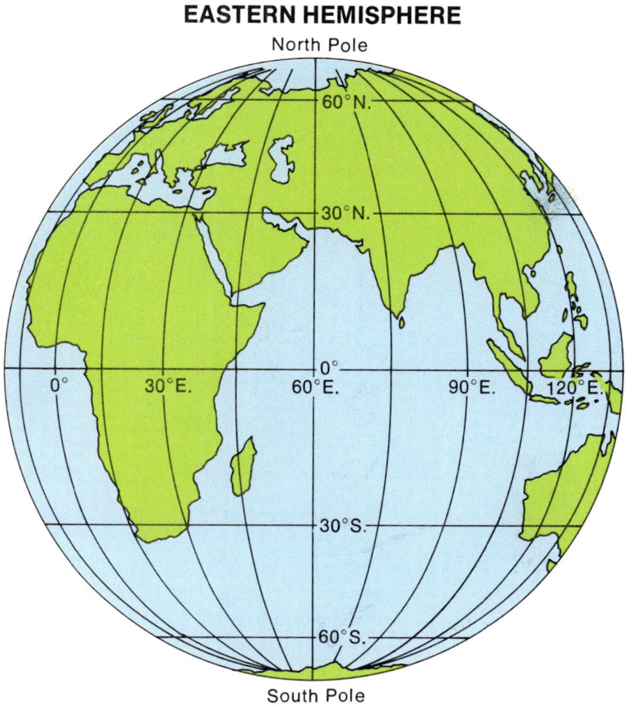

the North Pole and the South Pole. It divides the globe into the Northern Hemisphere and the Southern Hemisphere. Why is each half called a hemisphere?

Look at the pictures of the globe on this page. Can you see that the globe is shown in two equal parts? But this globe has not been cut along the equator. It is not separated into a northern half and a southern half.

Instead, this globe has been divided along a line running through the North Pole and the South Pole.

If you cut a globe this way, what are the two hemispheres called? Why? In which hemisphere is the United States?

Word List

This word list is a "little dictionary" containing the important words in this book. It includes all the words printed in *italics,* or slanting type, and the names of people and places that may be new to you. The meaning and the pages on which the word appears are given for each word. In most cases, you will find only the meanings that the words have in this book. You can look in a large dictionary for other meanings of these words.

Most of the words have been respelled to help you pronounce them correctly. The marks on the words below show how to pronounce the different letters. Those syllables printed in dark, thick type should be given the greatest force.

a as in hat	ē as in wē	ō as in nō	ou as in loud	ə = a as in a **go**
ā as in māke	i as in tin	ô as in côrd	u as in dust	ə = e as in **a** gent
ä as in cär	ī as in kīte	oo as in cook	ū as in hūge	ə = i as in **fam** i ly
e as in let	o as in top	o͞o as in to͞o	ũ as in fũr	ə = o as in **king** dom
		oi as in soil		ə = u as in **faith** ful

A

adobe (ə **dō** bē): a building material made from clay and straw, 258. *Pictures*, 259, 260, 262

apartment (ə **pärt** mənt) house: a building where many families live in separate apartments, 80, 111

Appalachian (a pə **lā** chē ən) Mountains: a mountain range in eastern United States, 134. *Map*, 134

Atlantic Ocean (at **lan** tik **ō** shən): the ocean dividing North and South America from Europe and Africa, 52

B

barter (**bär** tər): to trade without using money, 108

basic needs (**bā** sik **nēdz**): things people must have in order to live, 18, 19, 21, 30, 76. *Pictures*, 18, 19

Basket Makers: some of the first people to live in the Southwest 2,000 years ago, 256–258, 261, 263

Banneker, Benjamin (**ban** ə kər, **ben** jə mən): a person who helped build Washington, D.C., 122, 125–127. *Picture*, 122

bog: wet, spongy ground, 71, 73. *Picture*, 72

border (**bôrd** ər): where one place stops and another begins, 194, 209

borough (**bur** ō): one of the five parts of New York City, 83, 111. *Map*, 83

C

canoes (kə **nōōz**): Indian boats made of stretched animal skins or the bark from birch trees, 49. *Picture*, 48

canyon (**kan** yən): a narrow valley with high, steep sides, usually with water running through it, 273

capital (**kap** ə təl): the city where the government of a country or state is located, 112, 115, 123, 124, 126, 140. *Pictures*, 114, 115, 116, 118, 119, 121, 129, 132. *Map*, 126

Capitol (**kap** ə təl): the building in Washington, D.C., where Congress meets, 115–117. *Pictures*, 114, 115, 128, 129. *Map*, 127

cardinal (**kärd** ə nəl) direction: one of the four main directions, north, east, south, west. *Map*, 4, 5.

cattle drive: the trip cowboys took with their cattle to places where the cattle could be shipped by railroad, 204, 205. *Pictures*, 202, 206

celebration (sel ə **brā** shən): a special occasion, 66, 70, 186. *Pictures*, 266, 268

ceremony (**ser** ə **mō** nē): special actions done on a special occasion, 254. *Pictures*, 257, 263, 265

D

district (**dis** trikt): part of a city, state, or country, 95, 96, 97, 99. *Pictures*, 96, 97, 98

drought (**drout**): a long time without water, 276

dugouts (**dug** outs): Indian boats made by hollowing out logs with sharp stones, 49

E

elected (i **lekt** əd): chosen by vote, 119, 140

Ellicott, Andrew (**el** ə kət, **an** drōō): one of the men who helped Pierre L'Enfant draw plans for the city of Washington, D.C., 125, 126

engineer (en jə **nēr**): a person who plans and builds railroads, bridges, and dams, 14

equator (i **kwā** tər): an imaginary line drawn around the globe that divides the globe into two equal parts, 304, 305

F

factories (**fac** tər ēz): buildings where things are made, 150, 155. *Picture*, 149

federal district (**fed** ər əl **dis** trikt): the part of a country that belongs to the whole country, 116, 140. *Map*, 126

flood (**flud**): a great flow of water over the land, 23, 24, 179, 180, 276. *Picture*, 23

flood plain (**flud plān**): the low land next to a river, 180

fuel (**fyū** əl): something that runs machines and heats buildings when burnt, 198, 199

future (**fū** chər): the time to come, 284, 285, 287

G

government (**guv** ərn mənt): all the people who make the laws and run the country, 124, 140, 237, 238. *Picture*, 129

governor (**guv** ər nər): an elected leader of a group of people, 262, 264

H

I

K

L

M

Mayflower Compact: the agreement the Pilgrims made on the Mayflower to follow their own laws in the New World, 55. *Picture*, 55

member of Congress (**kong** grəs): one of the country's elected leaders who helps make the laws, 128, 132, 133, 140, 287. *Picture*, 129

mesa (**mā** sə): a small, high, flat area of land, 247, 252

Mexico (**mex** i kō): a country in North America just south of the United States, 129, 130, 209, 213, 214

mission (**mish** ən): old Spanish settlement and church in the Southwest, 210, 215. *Picture*, 211

Mississippi (mis ə **sip** ē) River: a large river in the United States that flows south from Minnesota to the Gulf of Mexico, 171, 172, 176–178, 183, 184. *Pictures*, 177, 179. *Map*, 178

monument (**mon** yə mənt): something built to remember a person or an event, 120. *Picture*, 120

mountains (**mount** tənz): high lands that rise steeply to peaks or points, 134–136, 245, 134, 299 . *Map*, 298, 299

N

natural gas: a substance that can be used as fuel, 198, 199

Navajo (**näv** ə hō): an Indian tribe in the Southwest, 226, 240–255, 261, 267, 268, 276. *Pictures*, 242, 243, 244, 247, 249, 250, 251, 252, 253, 254

neighborhood (**nā** bər hood): a community inside a city, 90–95, 102, 111. *Pictures*, 90, 91, 92, 95

New England (**ing** glənd): the six states in the northeastern United States: Connecticut, Maine, Massachusetts, New Hampshire, Rhode Island, and Vermont, 36. *Picture*, 36

O

orchard (**ôr** chərd): land on which fruit trees grow, 163, 166. *Picture*, 162

P

pages (**pā** jəz): boys and girls 14 to 18 years old who help out with different jobs when Congress meets in Washington, D.C., 132, 140, 287. *Picture*, 132

Pecos (**pā** kōs) River: river that runs through eastern New Mexico and Texas, 201, 223

Pilgrims (**pil** grimz): people who sailed on the *Mayflower* from England to the New World in 1620, 51–70, 109. *Pictures*, 53, 54, 56, 57, 58, 59, 61, 63, 64, 67

piñon (**pin** yōn): a small desert tree, bearing seeds that can be eaten, 243

pioneer (pī ə **nir**): someone who leads the way into new land, 16, 17, 129, 220, 229, 231. *Pictures*, 16, 40

plains (**plānz**): flat stretches of land, 223. *Map*, 299

planned city: a city built from plans carefully worked out ahead of time, 123, 124, 240. *Maps*, 126, 127, 272

plantation (plan **tā** shən): a large farm that grows crops such as cotton, rice, or tobacco, 159. *Picture*, 159

plateau (pla **tō**): flat land, higher than a plain, with steep sides, 298, 299

Plimouth Plantation (**pli** məth plan **tā** shən): a copy of the community built by the Pilgrims in 1620, 56–60. *Pictures*, 56, 63

Plymouth (**pli** məth): the first home of the Pilgrims in the New World in 1620, 52. *Pictures*, 53, 54

port: a harbor where ships can load and unload goods, 87, 111, 183, 192. *Pictures*, 86, 87, 168, 182, 188, 189

Potomac (pə **tō** mək) River: the river separating the District of Columbia and Maryland from Virginia, 124, 125

pottery (**pot** ə rē): bowls, pots, and other dishes made of clay, 257, 258, 266, 267. *Pictures*, 252, 256, 257

President (**prez** ə dənt): the chief elected leader of the United States, 117, 119, 140. *Pictures*, 120, 125

pueblo (**pweb** lō): a Pueblo Indian village built of adobe and stone, 258–269. *Pictures*, 259, 260, 262, 267

Pueblo (**pweb** lō) Indians: several Indian tribes in southwestern United States, 258–269, 276. *Pictures*, 260, 263, 264, 265, 266, 267, 268

R

S

suburb (**sub** ərb): a small town or village on the edge of a large city or town, 106, 111. *Picture*, 106

subway (**sub** wā): a railroad that runs underground, 88, 89, 111. *Picture*, 88

T

tall tale: a make-believe story, 201, 202, 205

textile mill (**tex** təl **mil**): a factory where thread is made into cloth, 136, 138, 140. *Picture*, 138

town meeting: a general meeting of the people living in the town, 32. *Picture*, 31

trade: the exchange of goods between people, 60, 248, 249, 250, 255. *Pictures*, 248, 249

transportation (trans pôr **tā** shən): the ways people use to move themselves or goods from one place to another, 47

transportation (trans pôr **tā** shən) center: a place to and from which goods are shipped, 147, 148, 150, 160, 212

tribes (**trībz**): groups of people sharing the same customs and beliefs, 42, 245, 263

truck farm: a farm where people grow vegetables to sell, 107–110. *Pictures*, 108, 109

turquoise (**tur** koiz): a sky-blue or greenish-blue stone. Also, that color, 250, 253. *Pictures*, 250, 254, 257

W

Washington (**wäsh** ing tən), D.C.: the capital of the United States, 112–133. *Pictures*, 114, 115, 118, 119, 128. *Maps*, 126, 127

Washington, George (**wäsh** ing tən, jôrj): 1732–1799, first President of the United States, 117, 120. *Picture*, 125

wigwam (**wig** wäm): an Indian house made of poles, covered with skins, barks, or grass, and rounded on top, 47. *Picture*, 46

Woodland Indians (**wood** lənd in dē ənz): groups of Indians who once lived in the woodlands in the eastern part of the United States, 42–45, 47–49, 51. *Pictures*, 42, 49

woodlands (**wood** ləndz): land covered with trees, 34, 42, 47. *Maps*, 143, 301

Acknowledgments

This book was prepared and produced by Educational Challenges, Inc., Alexandria, VA.

Front Cover and Title Page: (left), Robert Phillips/The Image Bank: (right), William Strede/Woodfin Camp. *Back Cover:* (left), Barbara Burnes/The Image Bank; (right), A. Devaney.

Unit One: 8, Chuck O'Rear/Woodfin Camp; 9 (left), Suzanne Szasz/Environmental Protection Agency Documerica (EPA); 9 (right), Dick Hanley/Photo Researchers; 10; Jack Lefkowitz; 11, Donald Gates; 12, Bullaty Lomeo, 13, Richard Frear/National Park Service (NPS); 14, Leonard Lee Rue/Shostal Assoc.; 15, Ray Manley/Shostal Assoc.; 16, National Archives; 18 (left), Soil Conservation Service (SCS); 18 (right), Bullaty Lomeo; 19, Robert Miller/Shostal Assoc.; 20, American Airlines; 22, Jack Lefkowitz; 23, SCS; 25 (left), United States Department of Agriculture (USDA); 25 (right), SCS; 28 (top left); W. B. Finch/Stock, Boston; 28 (top right,) Van Bucher/Photo Researchers; 28 (bottom), L. M. Dehnel; 30 (top), Bullaty Lomeo; 30 (bottom), USTS, 31 (top), Tom Hollyman/Photo Researchers; 31 (bottom left), John Messina/EPA; 31 (bottom right), Dick Hanley/Photo Researchers; 34, Jack Lefkowitz; 35, Donald Gates; 36, Peter M. Miller/Photo Researchers; 37, Katherine Kahn; 39, Bullaty Lomeo; 40, Van Bucher/Photo Researchers; 42, Courtesy of the American Museum of Natural History; 43, Jack Lefkowitz; 44, Katherine Kahn; 46 (top), Bill Arps/Photri; 46 (bottom), Bill Arps/Photri; 48, Frederick Remington/Roloc; 49, Katherine Kahn; 50 (top), Artie Grace/Sygma; 50 (bottom), Artie Grace/Sygma; 53, Hal Neilson/Shostal Assoc.; 54, A. Moran/ Courtesy of the Pilgrim Society; 56, Hal Neilson/Shostal Assoc.; 57, Farrell Grehan/Photo Researchers; 58, Hal Neilson/Shostal Assoc.; 59, Hal Neilson/Shostal Assoc.; 61, Michael Philip Manheim/Photo Researchers; 62, Katherine Kahn; 63, Plimoth Plantation; 64, *The Hornbook, Inc.;* 67, Michael Philip Manheim/Photo Researchers; 68-69, Katherine Kahn; 70, USDA; 72 (top), Dick Hanley/Photo Researchers, 72 (bottom), USDA.

Unit Two: 76, Bullaty Lomeo; 77 (left), Bruce Davidson/Photo Researchers; 77 (right), Roloc; 78, Jack Lefkowitz; 79, Donald Gates; 80, Bullaty Lomeo; 81, USTS; 82 (left), Roloc; 82 (right), Photri; 83, Jack Lefkowitz; 85, American Airlines; 86 (left), American Airlines; 86 (right), USTS; 87, Photri; 88, Jeffrey Jay Foxx/Woodfin Camp; 90, Suzanne Szasz/EPA; 91 (left), Eric Carlé/Shostal Assoc.; 91 (right), Bullaty Lomeo; 92 (left), Suzanne Szasz/EPA; 92 (right), Bullaty Lomeo; 93, Le Roy Woodson/Woodfin Camp; 94, John Lei/Stock, Boston; 95, Suzanne Szasz/EPA; 96 (left), Russell Dian; 96 (right), Sylvia Johnson/Woodfin Camp; 97 (left), USTS; 97 (right), USTS; 98, Sonja Bullaty/Bullaty Lomeo; 100, American Airlines; 101 (top), Suzanne Szasz/EPA; 101 (bottom), Sonja

Bullaty/Bullaty Lomeo; 103, USTS; 104 (top), Ralph Looney/Shostal Assoc.; 104 (bottom left), Don Schuhart/SCS; 104 (bottom right), USTS; 105 (top), Maureen Carlé/Shostal Assoc.; 105 (bottom left), Eric Carlé/Shostal Assoc.; 105 (bottom right), NPS; 106, Photri; 107, James A. Sugar/Woodfin Camp; 108, David Warren/USDA; 109, SCS; 110, SCS; 112, Jack Lefkowitz; 113, Donald Gates; 114 Photri; 115, Fred Bell/NPS; 116, Roloc; 118, NPS; 119, John Krowt/NPS; 121, Jack Rottier/NPS; 122, Roloc; 124, Jon Allen/Photo Researchers; 125, Library of Congress; 126, Library of Congress; 127, Jack Lefkowitz; 128, L. M. Dehnel; 129, United States Capitol Historical Society; 130, Paul Salmon; 132, U.S. House of Representatives; 134, Jack Lefkowitz; 135, Paul Salmon; 137, Photri; 138, Warren Uzzle/Photo Researchers

Unit Three: 142, Jim Amos/Photo Researchers; 143 (left), Maury Englander/Shostal Assoc.; 143 (right), Roloc; 144, Jack Lefkowitz; 145, Donald Gates; 146, Van Bucher/Photo Researchers; 147, William S. Weems/Woodfin Camp; 148; Roloc; 149, Lockheed; 151, Paul Salmon; 153, Atlanta Chamber of Commerce; 154 (left), Michael Philip Manheim/Photo Researchers; 154 (right), Roloc; 155 (left), Jay Leviton/Photo Researchers; 155 (right), William S. Weems/Woodfin Camp; 157, United Press International; 159, Library of Congress; 160 (top), Roloc, 160 (bottom), USTS; 161 (top left), Roloc; 161 (top right), United Airlines; 161 (bottom left), Van Bucher/Photo Researchers; 161 (bottom right), Roloc; 162, Joe Munroe/Photo Researchers; 163 (top), Agricultural Marketing Service (AMS), USDA; 163 (bottom), Gene Alexander/SCS; 164-65, Paul Salmon; 166, AMS USDA; 168, Roloc; 169, Donald Gates; 170, USTS; 171, Jack Lefkowitz; 172, Bradley Smith/Photo Researchers, 173 (left), USTS; 173 (right), USTS; 175 (top), Library of Congress; 175 (bottom), Bradley Smith/Photo Researchers; 176, National Archives; 177 (left), Jack Zehrt; 177 (right), USDA; 178, Jack Lefkowitz; 179, Ray Manley/Shostal Assoc.; 180, George Suyeoka; 182, Ray Manley/Shostal Assoc.; 184, USTS; 185, USTS; 186, Louisiana Tourist Development Commission; 187, Chuck O'Rear/Woodfin Camp; 188 (left), Craig Aurness/Woodfin Camp; 188 (middle), USTS; 188 (top), Hella Hammid/Photo Researchers; 189 (top left), Alvis Upitis/Shostal Assoc.; 189 (top right), Michael Philip Manheim/Photo Researchers; 189 (bottom), Rene Pauli/Shostal Assoc.; 190, Paul Salmon; 192, Photri; 194, Jack Lefkowitz; 195, Donald Gates; 196, Kurt Scholz/Shostal Assoc.; 197, George Suyeoka; 198, Chuck O'Rear/Woodfin Camp; 200, Library of Congress; 201, USDA; 203, Bill Gillette/EPA; 204, Denver Public Library, Western History Division; 206, Joe Munroe/Photo Researchers; 208 (top), Jack Lefkowitz, 208 (bottom), David Cain/Photo Researchers; 210, National Archives, 211, Joe Munroe/Photo Researchers; 212 (left), Bruce Roberts/Photo Researchers; 212 (right), Chuck O'Rear/Woodfin Camp; 213, Fred Mang, Jr./NPS; 214 (left), Fred Mang, Jr./NPS; 214 (right), Fred Mang, Jr./NPS; 215 (left), Fred Mang, Jr./NPS; 215 (right), Fred Mang, Jr., NPS.

Unit Four: 218, Fred E. Mang, Jr./NPS; 219 (left), Chuck O'Rear/Woodfin Camp; 219 (right), Van Bucher/Photo Researchers; 220, Jack Lefkowitz; 221, Donald Gates; 222 (left), Bullaty Lomeo; 222 (right), USTS; 223, (left), Jim Amos/Photo Researchers; 223 (right), Cecil Stoughton/NPS; 224 (left), M. Woodbridge Williams/NPS; 224 (right), Richard Frear/NPS; 226, Margaret Granitaas/Photo Researchers; 227, USTS; 228, USTS; 230, R. S. Uzzell III; 232, M. Woodbridge Williams/NPS; 233, Don Schuhart/SCS; 234, Gene Alexander/SCS; 235, Gene Alexander/SCS; 236 (top), Roloc; 236 (bottom left), Russell Dian; 236 (bottom right), Photri; 237 (left), Alan Felix/Shostal Assoc.; 237 (right), Photri; 238 (left), SCS; 238 (right), SCS; 240, USTS; 241, Donald Gates; 242, Michal Heron/Woodfin Camp; 243 (left), Richard Frear/NPS;. 243 (right), Paolo Koch/Photo Researchers; 244, USDA; 246, Don Schuhart/SCS; 247, Don Getsug/Photo Researchers; 248, Photri; 249 (left), NPS; 249 (right), The Squash Blossom, Ltd., Highland Park, IL/James L. Ballard; 250, Adam Woolfitt/Woodfin Camp; 251, Photri; 252 (left), Gianni Tortoli/Photo Researchers; 252 (right), USTS, 253 (left), Photri; 253 (right), Fred E. Mang, Jr./NPS; 254 (left), Michal Heron/Woodfin Camp; 254 (right), Roloc; 256, Museum of the American Indian; 257, USTS; 259 (top left), USTS; 259 (top right), Michal Heron/Woodfin Camp; 259 (bottom), USTS, 260, Myron Wood/Photo Researchers; 262, Fred E. Mang, Jr./NPS; 263, USDA; 264 (top), USDA; 264 (bottom), USTS; 265 (left), Michal Heron/Woodfin Camp; 265 (right), USDA; 266, Adam Woolfitt/Woodfin Camp; 267, Adam Woolfitt/Woodfin Camp; 268, Dan Budnik/Woodfin Camp; 270, George Halt/Woodfin Camp; 271, Donald Gates; 272, Jack Lefkowitz; 273, Terry Eiler/EPA; 274, SCS; 275 (left), Photri; 275 (right), Porterfield-Chickering/Photo Researchers; 276 (left), Richard Frear/NPS; 276 (right), Don Schuhart/SCS; 277, Carlos Elmer/Shostal Assoc.; 279, David Brownell/Woodfin Camp; 280 (upper left), Chuck O'Rear/Woodfin Camp; 280 (lower left), L. M. Dehnel; 280 (upper right), Larry Mulvihill/Photo Researchers; 280 (lower right), Arizona Office of Tourism; 281 (upper left), Buddy Mays/Photo Researchers; 281 (center left), Elihu Blotnick/Woodfin Camp; 281 (top right), Tom McHugh/Photo Researchers; 281 (lower left), Porterfield-Chickering/Photo Researchers; 281 (bottom right), Farrell Grehan/Photo Researchers; 282 (left), James A. Sugar/Photo Researchers; 282 (lower right), Adam Woolfitt/Woodfin Camp; 282 (top right), Adam Woolfitt/Woodfin Camp; 283 (top left), L. Eiler/EPA Documerica; 283 (bottom right), Adam Woolfitt/Woodfin Camp; 285 (left), Elihu Blotnick/Woodfin Camp; 286, R. S. Uzzell III.